T0301117

Your Baby's First Year

In 2002, Louenna Hood graduated from the prestigious Norland College in Bath, Somerset, which has trained elite nannies for 130 years. Over almost two decades, she has nannied over 100 children, including the offspring of celebrities and royalty, and has worked in countries across the globe, including Dubai, Australia, America and Sweden. Qualifying as a maternity nurse a decade ago – a decision that led her into freelance work – cemented Louenna as a go-to support for many high-profile new parents. Then in March 2020, as her childcare duties scaled back during the pandemic, Louenna took her career to the next level, by making her childcare services completely inclusive via a dedicated parent support app, The Louenna App. A one-stop-shop for childcare, the app covers every possible parenting topic from feeding, bathing and changing, to sleep routines, potty training and language development. Originally from Norfolk, Louenna currently lives in Newmarket in Cambridgeshire with her daughter.

Your Baby's First Year

A day-by-day guide

LOUENNA HOOD

Louenna graduated from Norland College in 2005 and her advice, views and guidance should not be taken as being endorsed by Norland or representative of its current training, research or advice on best practice.

Copyright © 2024 Louenna Hood

The right of Louenna Hood to be identified as the Author of the Work has been asserted by her in accordance with the Copyright, Designs and Patents Act 1988.

First published in 2024 by Headline Home
an imprint of Headline Publishing Group

2

Apart from any use permitted under UK copyright law, this publication may only be reproduced, stored, or transmitted, in any form, or by any means, with prior permission in writing of the publishers or, in the case of reprographic production, in accordance with the terms of licences issued by the Copyright Licensing Agency.

Illustrations copyright © 2024 Hannah Riordan

Cataloguing in Publication Data is available from the British Library.

Hardback ISBN 9781035409655
eISBN 9781035409679

Designed and typeset by EM&EN
Printed and bound in Great Britain by Clays Ltd, Elcograf S.p.A.

Headline's policy is to use papers that are natural, renewable and recyclable products and made from wood grown in well-managed forests and other controlled sources. The logging and manufacturing processes are expected to conform to the environmental regulations of the country of origin.

HEADLINE PUBLISHING GROUP
An Hachette UK Company
Carmelite House
50 Victoria Embankment
London EC4Y 0DZ

www.headline.co.uk
www.hachette.co.uk

For my little Alice Valentine,

Love Mummy x

The information in this book is not intended to be a substitute for medical advice or medical treatment. You are advised to consult a midwife or doctor on any matters relating to your baby's or your own health, and in particular on any matters that may require diagnosis or medical attention. Any use of the information in this book is made on the reader's good judgement and is the reader's sole responsibility.

Contents

Introduction

Congratulations! After months of wondering there's nothing more exciting than holding your baby and looking into their precious little face!

Bringing your baby home comes with a huge mix of emotions – there's so much joy and love, but it can also be exhausting as you recover from birth. My top tips for the first few weeks would be to focus on establishing a good feeding pattern and mastering the art of swaddling your baby when they sleep!

I hope this book of daily wins helps you to enjoy each day with your little one.

About me

I am a qualified Norland Nanny and Maternity Nurse who has cared for more than 100 children over the past two decades, travelling the world with families, including high-profile and royal families.

Having been a go-to support for many parents over the years, I wanted to help others on their most important journey by making my expertise accessible to all via a dedicated parenting support, the Louenna App. Through my website, I offer one-to-one support for parents who would like personalised expert advice from my dedicated team.

In July 2023, I became a mum myself after adopting a baby girl. We live in Suffolk along with our mini dachshund Tess, where I oversee the running of the Louenna App, the nanny agency Louenna's Nannies and my new enterprise: Louenna's Bump, Birth and Baby Antenatal Classes. This book is a distillation of all I have learned from my many years of supporting new parents and their little ones.

How the book works

I want this book to be a daily source of inspiration, to help guide you through the exciting yet sometimes overwhelming first year of your baby's life. By giving you tips that are specific to your little one's stage of development, I hope it encourages you to have the confidence to enjoy lots of special moments together.

In the beginning of this book you will find all of my tips surrounding baby basic care such as changing a nappy, holding your baby, feeding and swaddling them.

There are five routines in the book that I would recommend following at the different stages of your little one's first year. By following the routines, your little one will have enough sleep and awake times during the day, ensuring they are happy and you all get the sleep that you need at night.

At the back of the book you will find an index for you to look up specific topics.

QR Codes

Finally, there are QR codes dotted throughout the book that lead to demonstration videos to help bring my advice to life. Open the camera app on your phone and hold it over the QR code until a link appears. Then follow the link to the video!

But before we go any further, let's start with your recovery from the birth . . .

Recovering from the Birth

First things first – you need to focus on helping your body to recover from the birth in these first few weeks, as well as looking after your baby. Here are some tips but do speak to your midwife or health visitor if you have any concerns about your physical or mental recovery.

Tips to help a vaginal birth recovery:

- Take arnica tablets to aid bruising from within.
- Have a bath or a shower once a day to stop infection.
- Add a couple of scoops of Epsom salts or a few drops of lavender oil, camomile, rosehip oil or tea tree oil to your bath for added healing and soothing.
- Use cushions for support when sitting down.
- Lie with a bag of frozen peas between your legs (making sure the bag is wrapped in a cloth or you have clothes on to prevent freezer burn) to reduce swelling.
- Keep a big bottle of room-temperature water by the loo that you can pour on yourself while peeing to take the sting away. Also consider peeing in the shower for the first few days if you are sore.
- Eat plenty of fibre and drink plenty of water to keep your bowel movements as soft as possible.

Tips to help C-section recovery:

- Be careful when you get up for the first time and make sure someone is there to help you. Your scar will feel sore so take your time.
- Unless told otherwise, it's important to start moving within twenty-four hours of your operation as this will help your recovery, release gas and start to get your bowels moving too.
- Try to air the wound twice per day once the dressing comes off; however, it does vary when this happens. Sometimes it is removed within a couple of days but it can be up to 5–7 days. Your midwife will advise you.
- Wear loose clothing that sits above your scar.
- Set an alarm to take your painkillers regularly, day and night.
- If you are suffering from wind, drinking peppermint tea or chewing gum will help reduce bloating and relieve discomfort.
- Eat plenty of fibre and drink plenty of water to keep your bowel movements as soft as possible.
- Use cushions for support when sitting down.
- Have a daily shower.

Baby Basics

So you have a baby! Now what?! Here are a few basics to get you started. Follow the link on page 20 to the QR code to watch my video demonstrating how to swaddle your baby.

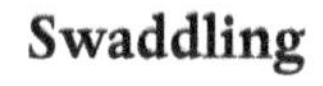

Swaddling

To swaddle your baby, fold a large muslin in half and lay it on a soft surface. Place your baby in the centre of the muslin, with their head clear of the material.

Place their arms down and bring one side of the muslin over your baby and tuck it underneath them on the opposite side.

Then bring the other side of the swaddle over your baby and wrap it underneath their back.

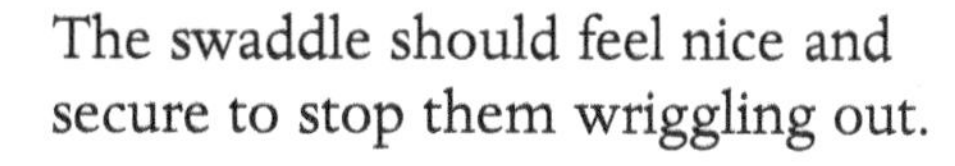

The swaddle should feel nice and secure to stop them wriggling out.

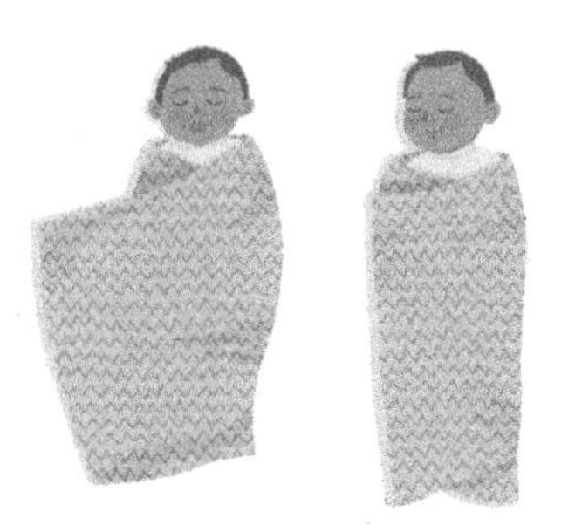

Make sure the swaddle starts from their shoulders and not the neck. Hips and legs should be left completely free, but the top of the swaddle creates security for babies who are used to being snug and warm in the womb.

Safe sleep advice

When you put your little one to sleep, always place them on their back and think 'feet to foot' (see illustration below). By placing their feet at the bottom of their cot, they aren't able to wriggle down and underneath any blankets which could pose a suffocation risk.

Always put your baby in a sleep space that has a firm mattress, is smoke-free, has no bumpers, is free from any toys and can't be reached by family pets.

Newborns can sleep in a cot from birth, rather than a Moses basket. The benefit of a Moses basket is that it is smaller in your bedroom and can easily be moved around the house if necessary. However, they do grow out of them within a few months so you could save money by using a cot from the very beginning.

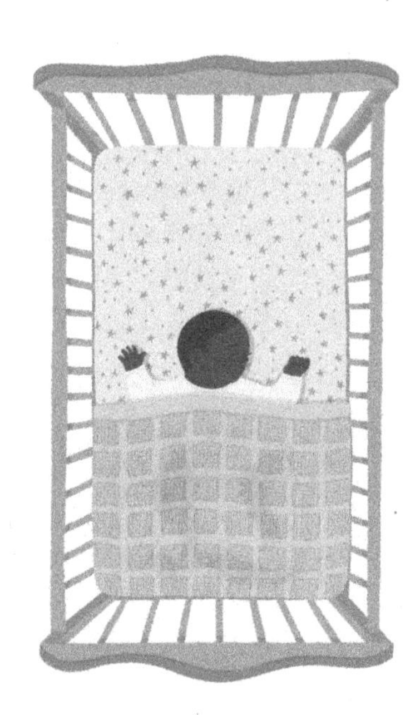

Co-sleeping

Co-sleeping is when your little one shares a bed with you. I personally never recommend co-sleeping: I feel it is unsafe due to loose covers and the risk of overheating and suffocation. I also don't feel anyone gets a proper night's sleep while co-sleeping.

If you do choose to co-sleep, please have a look at the advice given by The Lullaby Trust to ensure you make it as safe an environment as possible for your baby.

Never co-sleep if:

- You or anyone else in the bed has consumed any alcohol
- You or anyone else in the bed is a smoker, drug user or has taken medication that could make them drowsy
- Your baby was premature or weighed less than 2.5kg (5½lbs) at birth

How to co-sleep safely:

- Keep any loose bedding and pillows away from your baby to avoid suffocation or overheating
- Always put your baby to sleep on their back
- Do not allow other children or pets into the bed
- Never leave your baby unattended
- Ensure your baby is safe in the bed by making sure they cannot fall out or become trapped anywhere

Breastfeeding

Recognising feeding cues

Your baby will show that they are ready to feed long before they start crying. Feeding cues to look for include:

- Mouth movements (licking lips and opening wide)
- Rooting or sucking fists and fingers
- Stretching
- Turning their head

You will be amazed at how in sync you are with your baby. It is likely you will naturally wake up at night around feed times and your breasts will feel larger or start to flow.

A calm baby will usually go to the breast contentedly. If your baby gets to the point of crying, they may refuse the breast even when they are hungry. This is why I suggest following a routine so that your baby avoids being 'hangry'!

How you can tell when a baby is sucking and swallowing

Babies aren't always taking in milk when they are at the breast. Try to make sure they are using their feed time to fill up and not using you as a comfort or dummy as this will mean they are hungry in an hour, and you will get sore.

You can tell your baby is swallowing when you hear them gulping their milk. When they swallow you can see muscles moving at their ears, and your baby's chin will drop down and make long, slow and deep movements.

If there is a lot of sucking, take them off the breast (see page 10), wake them up by winding or changing their nappy and relatch. Effective feeding is done in bursts of around three to four sucks then a swallow. If you hear a clicking noise when they are feeding take them off and change their position to encourage a better latch.

A good latch

A good latch is important so that your baby stimulates the milk glands, and doesn't make you sore. Hold your baby's head so that their nose is level with your nipple. Put your nipple on the top of your baby's mouth to encourage them to open their mouth widely. The wider they open their mouth, the easier it is to get a good latch.

When their mouth is open at the widest, aim your nipple at the roof of their mouth; your baby's chin should be the first thing to touch your breast. This may take some practice, as you have to be quite fast!

Their bottom lip should cover the whole underneath part of your areola, with their top lip scooped over your nipple, so your whole nipple is drawn to the back of your baby's mouth by their soft palate. Your baby's head should be tilting slightly back, with a small gap between their nose and your breast. If your baby's nose is squashed into your breast, or they do not take enough breast tissue into their mouth, your nipple will rest on their hard palate and you will likely feel a pinching or biting, which can end in sore nipples. If you still feel pain after the first thirty seconds, take your baby off and try re-latching.

If your baby's latch is too shallow, it can slow down your milk flow, prolonging the feeds. It may also lead to your baby being hungry more frequently, as they might not be draining the breast fully in order to get to the fattier milk. Other side effects include blocked ducts and a low milk supply.

If you are concerned about your baby's latch, speak to your midwife or a lactation consultant. Sometimes, not being able to achieve a good latch can be down to your baby having a tongue-tie (see page 14). Have an expert check if you think this could be the problem.

Remember, each mum and baby has a unique combination of anatomy, so if you are having problems, it's best to speak to a breastfeeding specialist who can give you individualised advice. Stay positive as these problems are often easy to sort so you can go on to have an enjoyable breastfeeding experience.

Taking your baby off the breast

Don't pull your baby off the breast, as this will be painful. Place your little finger in the side of your baby's mouth to release the seal and they will then come off the breast easily without damaging your nipple.

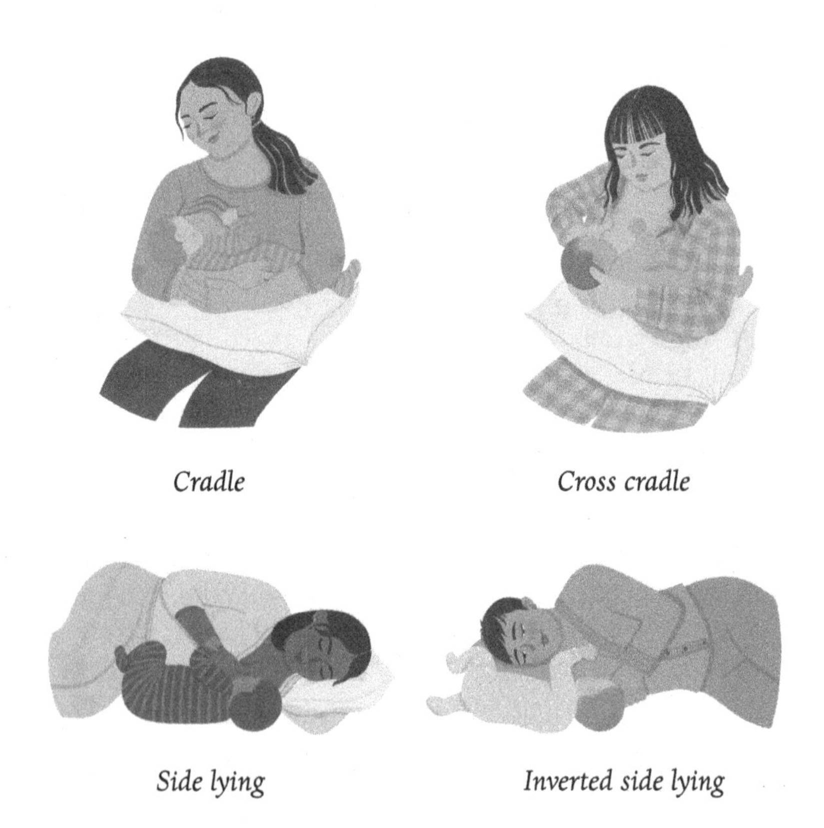

Cradle *Cross cradle*

Side lying *Inverted side lying*

Which breast first?

Some babies get everything they need from one breast, whilst others may need an extra top-up from the other breast or they may need two full breasts with every feed. Whatever your baby prefers, alternate which breast you start each feed with to prevent engorgement and help regulate your supply evenly. When you are sleep-deprived this can be really tricky to remember, so use the feeding timer on my Louenna App to record and remind you which side to start feeding from next.

Football hold

Australian hold

Side-lying cradle

Back lying

Is my baby getting enough milk?

Your baby is getting enough milk if they are satisfied until the next feed. You will know if your little one is satisfied if they sleep well in-between feeds and are happy and content until their next feed time. They shouldn't need to feed any more than every three hours from the start of each feed. If they do, think about trying to up your milk supply by expressing after every feed, resting, staying hydrated and eating well.

Breast or bottle?

If you find you can't breastfeed your baby or you choose not to, don't let anyone make you feel bad about it!

The World Health Organisation (WHO) recommends exclusively breastfeeding for at least six months but for some women this isn't possible. The good news is that babies thrive on bottle feeding, just as they do by being breastfed.

I firmly believe that fed is best, and it's not always breast is best for every family. If you're not happy breastfeeding, then don't feel guilty. Your happiness and wellbeing are two of the most important things when it comes to keeping your baby happy and well.

It's your baby and your body. I have looked after dozens of babies who weren't breastfed and they have become happy, healthy and thriving children. You can't walk into a classroom of five-year-olds and identify which ones were breastfed and which were raised on formula!

You may choose to express your breast milk and give it to your baby in a bottle. You may choose to breastfeed your baby and offer formula milk top-ups. You may choose to feed your baby exclusively with formula milk. I have cared for babies who are fed in all these ways, and as long as it's a decision made by the parents without pressure from others, then they are all feeding methods by which a baby will thrive.

How to change a nappy

When changing your baby's nappy, make sure you have everything you need before you start. Place your baby on a comfortable surface, such as a changing mat, and cover any plastic surfaces that their skin will be exposed to with a muslin, disposable mat or towel to make sure they don't get cold. Also, if your little one wees on a plastic mat, it will run everywhere rather than being absorbed by material.

Talk to your baby whilst you are changing them and place a reassuring hand on their tummy if they get startled when their nappy comes off. Undo the two tapes from the nappy and hold your baby's legs up so that you can wipe any poo from the front of the nappy area to the bottom, and put the wipe straight into the dirty nappy. Clean your baby's bottom thoroughly, remembering to wipe front to back if you have a little girl.

When the area is clean, slide the nappy out from underneath and discard into a nappy sack or nappy bin. Pat and dry their bottom with a tissue or towel. If you have time, let your baby have a kick around without their nappy on so that the skin gets a chance to breathe. Open up the clean nappy and place the tabs underneath at the back. The tabs should be fastened tight enough not to have a gaping hole at the front, but not too tight so that your baby is uncomfortable. Finally, pull out the fans around the legs to prevent leaks.

Umbilical cord care

Keep the umbilical cord clean by using a cotton pad and cooled boiled water to gently wipe away any dried blood around the area.

Place the nappy tabs below the cord so it doesn't rub or cause the cord to come off too soon. Depending on how the clamp sits, you might want to fold the nappy over the top or tuck it underneath – whichever looks the most comfortable.

It is normal for the umbilical area to look a little raw for a couple of days but if it is swollen, red, weeping or smelly, contact your midwife.

The cord will often fall away in the nappy or sometimes it floats off in the bath! When it comes off, wrap the cord in a used nappy and discard, unless you want to keep it in a keepsake box.

Tongue-tie

Tongue-tie is defined as restricted tongue movements caused by the frenulum – the piece of skin attaching the tongue to the base of the mouth – being short and tight, which can make it more difficult for them to feed.

A doctor should have checked for tongue-tie in the routine check before you leave hospital but it is often missed and only becomes apparent when your baby has problems latching and feeding.

Here are some signs to watch for:

- Inability to stick out the tongue or move it freely
- Cracked, bleeding, blistered or damaged nipples
- Nipples appear flat/squashed after feeding
- Breastfeeding is painful on an ongoing basis
- Difficulty latching and feeding
- The tongue appears heart-shaped when the baby sticks it out
- Baby makes a clicking sound when feeding
- Baby's mouth looks small on the breast
- Baby isn't gaining sufficient weight
- Long feed times such as one hour plus and baby still isn't satisfied
- Baby is very windy, producing green stools or generally unsettled and fractious

Consult your midwife or health visitor if you are concerned that your baby has a tongue-tie as it can be easily fixed with a minor procedure. No anaesthetic is used, although your baby will cry for a few seconds, which is more to do with you having to keep their head still while the process takes place than because of any pain. There is usually hardly any blood – sometimes none. Encourage your baby to suck straight away afterwards (have a bottle prepared if bottle feeding) and they will forget about the ordeal within a minute.

In very rare cases, tongue-ties can grow back.

Winding

Here are some winding positions for your baby.

Over your shoulder

Sitting on your lap

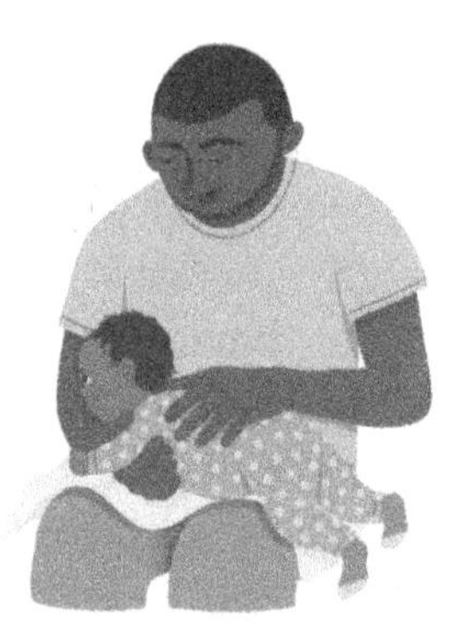

Lying on your lap

Tiger in the tree hold (see page 108)

So, now we've covered the basics, let's start your journey through your baby's first year!

Day 1

FACT Today, your baby will pass their first poo: meconium. Meconium is dark green, almost black, and looks like sticky tar – not what you'd expect! Meconium is composed of things your baby has ingested in the womb, including dead skin cells; remains of the hair that once covered them; mucus; amniotic fluid; bile; and water. Your baby will usually only have one or two dirty nappies in the first couple of days but because of its consistency, it's quite hard to wipe off!

FOOD FOR THOUGHT Allow your baby to latch and suckle during skin-to-skin contact in their first twenty-four hours after birth. Some babies may want to suckle for long periods, so remember to switch between breasts and get help with positioning and latching. It is normal for babies to only want two to three breastfeeds in the first twenty-four hours, as they may be sleepy after the birth. After the feed, cuddle your baby and comfort them by rhythmic patting and they should settle. If your baby is not latching, don't worry; it's a learning process for both of you. Take your time and it will happen. Try not to get upset or anxious – continue your skin-to-skin contact and ask for help from a midwife.

TIP It may be painful when you pee for the first time after birth, especially if you have had stitches. Drinking plenty of water dilutes your urine and can make it sting less.

ACTIVITY Enjoy skin-to-skin contact with your baby; it's a wonderful bonding time for you both. Babies find the warmth of your skin and the rhythm of your heartbeat really comforting and are more likely to feed if they are relaxed and happy.

Day 2

FACT In early pregnancy, your breasts produce colostrum, the first milk available to your baby after birth. It is much thicker than the breast milk which will follow and is usually a deep yellow. It's concentrated, nutritious and full of antibodies, so your baby will only need a small amount at each feed. The main role of colostrum is to kick-start your baby's immune system. It also acts as a natural laxative to help your baby clear out their first poo/meconium.

FOOD FOR THOUGHT Even though your baby might be happy to continue sleeping, don't let them go more than three to four hours between feeds. This means you will need to wake them to feed sometimes! Make yourself comfortable and get something to eat and drink before starting the feeding, changing and winding cycle. For the next few days your baby may be very sleepy and just want to eat and snooze; however, some babies are hungry and restless. You may need to feed a hungry baby more regularly but try to have breaks in between feeding so that you don't get exhausted and you give baby time to sleep.

HOW TO Practise changing your baby's nappy at every feed time, remembering to untuck the frill around your baby's legs which will help avoid leaks. Follow the link on this QR code to watch my video demonstration.

ACTIVITY Get a dose of fresh air, even if it means just sitting by an open window for half an hour. Half an hour of sunlight exposure (regardless of the weather) will boost your serotonin levels.

Day 3

If you are feeling emotional today, it's totally expected and due to your hormone levels changing. Ride the wave and cry to family and friends if you need to; it's all normal and won't last for long.

FACT If you notice your baby's skin has a yellow look to it, they may have jaundice. Jaundice is due to an immature liver function and causes a yellowing of the skin and whites of the eyes from bilirubin – a substance that forms after red blood cells break down – building up in the blood. It usually develops two to three days after birth and varies in severity from a yellowing of the palms of the hands and soles of the feet to a deeper yellow skin and eye whites. Symptoms can also include dark yellow urine (a baby's urine should be colourless) and pale-coloured poo. Jaundice is normal: it is estimated that six out of ten newborns develop it within the first few days of life. If you think your baby may have it, mention it to your midwife.

Babies with jaundice will often be quite sleepy and might have to be woken for feeding but to help treat jaundice at home you should feed your baby every three hours. Let your baby sleep in natural sunlight, near a window or outside in the pram, as the light on the skin helps to break down the bilirubin. However, be careful not to overheat or expose your baby to direct sunlight.

FOOD FOR THOUGHT It's more than likely your milk will come in today (it might be tomorrow). You'll notice you feel fuller, your baby will feed for longer periods and hopefully be more satisfied after their feed. There will be milk in your baby's mouth when they come off the breast and it's a thinner and whiter consistency than colostrum. If your breasts become engorged and uncomfortable when your milk comes in, a warm flannel used as a compress will help, along with a warm shower or bath.

Day 4

Between feeds, when your baby is happy, I advise putting them down in their bed so that they have time to relax and go into a deep restful sleep (see page 6 for how to put your baby down safely). The times between feeds are short so make the most of having your hands free for an hour. I believe this is healthy for everyone – even if you do spend the whole hour just gazing at your sleeping baby!

TIP Keep the umbilical cord clean by using a cotton pad and cooled boiled water to gently wipe away any dried blood around the area. Place the nappy tabs below the cord so it doesn't rub or cause the cord to come off too soon. Depending on how the clamp sits, you might want to fold the nappy over the top or tuck it underneath – whichever looks the most comfortable.

It is normal for the umbilical area to look a little raw in places for a couple of days but if you think it looks swollen and/or red, or if it is weeping or smelly, contact your midwife. The cord will often fall away in the nappy or bath! Once it comes off, wrap the cord in a used nappy and discard, unless you want to keep it in a keepsake box.

FACT Babies are born with a natural startle reflex, called the Moro reflex. This means that when they are disturbed by a noise or a feeling of falling, they jerk their arms and legs out. If your baby is swaddled they just re-settle because the movement is minimal, whereas if they aren't swaddled they often hit themselves in the face and start wriggling until they wake because they need the reassurance of being snug.

HOW TO Follow the link on this QR code to watch my video demonstrating how to swaddle your baby.

Day 5

You might be starting to get requests from family and friends to come and visit. If you feel like you're not up to it then don't feel bad for putting people off. This is your time to recover and bond with your baby.

Over the next couple of days, your midwife will visit and do a blood spot test – also known as the heel prick test – to check that your baby hasn't got sickle cell disease, cystic fibrosis, congenital hypothyroidism, or any inherited metabolic diseases. This comprises pricking your baby's heel and squeezing four drops of blood onto a special card. It's not too distressing for a baby but I always make sure they are warm and cosy and put an extra pair of socks or booties on their feet for an hour before the midwife arrives, so blood comes to the surface of the skin easily. If your baby is distressed by the heel prick, give them lots of cuddles and make a soothing, shushing noise. You can also feed them to give comfort.

FACT Your baby's tummy has gone from the size of a hazelnut to the size of an apricot in just a few days! So every day they should be able to take a little bit more milk at each feed.

FOOD FOR THOUGHT During the night feeds, have a snack to keep your energy levels up. An oat or cereal bar is perfect as it keeps your sugar levels consistent.

ACTIVITY Take your baby for a short walk in the pram today, even if this is just into your garden, if you have one. Swaddle your baby and put them into the pram after they have fed and been winded. Fresh air is so beneficial for both of you – I truly believe babies sleep better when they have had fresh air during the day.

Day 6

If you are breastfeeding, you may find your nipples are getting sore and/or cracked. Nipple creams help to prevent dry, cracked and painful nipples. Most creams are made using lanolin and are safe for baby to feed from so there is no need for you to wash it off before feeding.

FOOD FOR THOUGHT Post-birth constipation is common and nothing to worry about. Try this Gut-Friendly Smoothie recipe to help regulate your bowel movements.

Ingredients
1 pear, peeled and cored
5 strawberries (frozen is best)
1 teaspoon honey
60ml prune juice
1 tablespoon flax seeds

To make the smoothie, simply whizz together the ingredients in a blender and serve.

FACT In the first two weeks after birth, it's normal for breastfed babies to lose up to 10 per cent of their birth weight. Waking your baby regularly for feeds will help them get back to their birth weight.

HOW TO If your baby is back up to their birth weight, start to bathe them each evening. The only time I wouldn't bathe a newborn is if they are premature or losing weight: babies use up energy in the bath, so in these cases I would wait a little while. You might find it easier to bathe your newborn at waist height rather than having to bend down to bath level. You can do this in the sink or in a baby bath.

Bath water should be a temperature of 38°C. I suggest using a bath thermometer but if you don't have one, use your elbow to check the water temperature isn't too hot.

Try not to submerge your baby's ears in the water. If water does get into them, tilt baby's head for the water to drain out while you're getting them dry and gently wipe around the ears with a towel.

I like to bathe babies and children every evening as part of their routine. Babies love a nice warm bath and it makes an enjoyable sensory experience which soothes them ready for bedtime.

Follow the link on this QR code to watch my video on how to bathe your newborn without straining your back.

1 Week Old

You may be experiencing night sweats. If you are, this is due to your body having lots of stored fluid which it needs to expel after birth. This happens because of low levels of oestrogen as your body adjusts to not being pregnant any more. You may need to change your bedsheets in the night because you have sweated so much. To stay cool, open the windows, place a fan near your bed, drink cold water, and wear loose cotton night clothes. The night sweats should start to decline after two weeks post-birth, but if they continue for longer than three weeks consult your doctor. Make sure you continue to drink lots of water to keep your bladder and kidneys healthy.

It's normal for newborns to cry when you change their nappy: you aren't doing anything wrong. It's because they don't like the sensation of suddenly being cold. Don't panic when they cry, they are not in any pain. Have the confidence to keep talking to them, placing a hand on their tummy, but don't rush the nappy change. It's really important to take the time to clean them properly. As soon as they're wrapped up again you can give them a cuddle and all will be forgotten.

FACT Research suggests that from the second trimester, babies are able to hear music while in the womb and may recognise familiar music once they are born. Try playing some music to them during their nappy changes and see if it calms them.

ACTIVITY Today, your task is to wash your hair so you feel refreshed and revived and ask someone to take a photograph of you with your baby. Newborns change so quickly and it's important to have these special memories to look back on.

Week 1 Day 1

Hopefully you are beginning to feel more like yourself again and recovering well. Try to start moving more and go for a longer walk with your baby, as movement will help your recovery.

If you had a C-section, try to expose your stitches to the air (see tips to help C-section recovery on page 4).

HOW TO It is a myth that breastfed babies don't need winding. All babies – breast and bottle fed – need to be winded at each feed. If they don't bring up their wind you will have a very cross baby on your hands, and if they take in more milk when they still have wind the chances are they will bring it all up again with a burp. A burp or a fart both count but usually babies will bring up more than one lot of wind at a time!

Winding breaks are good to let your baby have a breather from feeding, and then they're ready to go again and take some more milk, creating a fulfilling feed.

A relaxed baby is much more likely to bring wind up. If they are crying or uptight their body won't relax and allow the wind to release. Use patting rhythms on their back or a gentle knee jog when holding your baby to put them into a little happy trance and their wind will come up much more easily!

Follow the link on this QR code to watch my video for all my winding tips.

TIP Babies find the rhythmic patting of winding therapeutic and relaxing. So when your baby is ready for a nap, try winding them again for a few minutes. This will relax them so they are ready to be swaddled and put down for a nice snooze . . .

Week 1 Day 2

It's a really nice idea to create a memory box for your baby that you can both treasure and look back on when they're older. Include things such as: scan photos, their hospital bracelet, a newspaper from the day they were born, a photo of you when you were pregnant, cards that were given to celebrate their arrival, their first babygrow and a size 1 nappy. They won't believe how tiny they once were!

Every month I am going to give you ideas of things you can add to your memory box.

FACT Babies often suffer from bad hand circulation. If they are swaddled when they sleep their hands stay nice and warm and they can't scratch themselves.

FOOD FOR THOUGHT You can buy effervescent multivitamin tablets that are packed with minerals and vitamins. Having one with your breakfast will help your energy levels throughout the day. When you are sleep-deprived, your immune system weakens so I advise new parents take multivitamins to help with this.

MINDFULNESS Your breath is your calming secret weapon. There will be moments that you feel stressed or overwhelmed as a parent but deep mindful breaths can work wonders. Next time you feel anxious, stop and take three deep breaths: in for six counts, hold for six and out for eight.

ACTIVITY Enjoy a warm bath or shower while your baby sleeps. Let them enjoy a good feed, wind them, swaddle them and tuck them in with a blanket. If there is someone else with you, ask them to watch your baby while you enjoy an hour to yourself.

Week 1 Day 3

I truly believe that babies thrive on a flexible and realistic routine from birth, and I always advise that one is established from the early weeks. It helps both of you. A routine means that your baby gets proper sleeps, full feeds, lots of cuddle time – and you can plan your day, and are able to get out and see people.

Routines are not there to be rigid, tie you to the house, or limit the amount of cuddles you have with your baby! A routine is there so that if you have a bad day – and this happens to everyone at times – or a day where you just have to go with the flow, you get back into the best rhythm for your baby the following morning. Without a routine in place, it is very easy for a baby to get into bad habits and for parents to feel overwhelmed with a never-ending sleep and feed routine.

It's very achievable for babies to sleep through the night by the time they are five months old. Sleep is vital for everyone in the family, and if you have a good night's sleep, you can deal with anything in the day. A routine will help you achieve this.

A good sleeping pattern offers huge benefits to everyone, and a good routine from day one will encourage this. I want everyone to enjoy their babies, and sleep-deprived parents don't enjoy the first year as much as they should.

Starting a routine may sound daunting but after a couple of days it will become second nature to you and your baby. I suggest you start your day at 7 a.m. with a feed, waking your baby if they are still sleeping. Then follow the routine timings for the rest of the day. I suggest working on a 7 a.m. to 7 p.m. routine because babies are best suited to the daylight hours.

See pages 28 to 29 for a detailed breakdown of my suggested timings for a newborn, Routine 1.

Routine 1

0 to 3 Months: The Three-Hourly Cycle

Throughout the routine I advise offering your baby a 'top-up' at each feed. This is because babies often get a second wind after a nappy change and winding. The top-up can be offered from your second breast if you are breastfeeding, or with a bottle if you are combination or bottle feeding.

7 a.m. Wake baby, if not already awake.

Feed, wind, change nappy, top and tail (wash their face and bottom) and get dressed. Try a short tummy time (if your baby's cord has fallen off) – see page 14. Offer a top-up feed.

8.30 a.m. Roughly 1.5 hours after waking, swaddle baby and put down for a nap. If you are going out shortly, put baby in their pram so that you don't have to transfer or disturb them.

10 a.m. Wake baby. Feed, wind, change nappy, offer a top-up feed.

11.30 a.m. Swaddle your baby and put them down for a nap.

1 p.m. Wake baby, feed, wind, nappy change, offer a top-up feed.

2.30 p.m. Swaddle your baby and put them down for a nap.

4 p.m. Wake baby, feed, wind, nappy change, offer a top-up feed within an hour.

5 p.m. Swaddle your baby and let them nap for an hour.

6 p.m. Wake baby after they've had an hour's sleep. If baby is fractious, let them feed for roughly half their feed (one side of breast, or half of their bottle), before winding them and letting them enjoy a nice bathtime. Then feed, wind and offer a top-up.

7.30 p.m. Swaddle and put baby to bed. In the first few weeks you may find this is your baby's fractious time, especially when establishing breastfeeding. The trick is not to let your baby get too overtired so that they can't settle. Let them cluster feed if they need, but try to wake them so they are feeding properly and are then satisfied enough to have a sleep before the next feed.

10 p.m. Wake baby, turn lights on and give baby a good feed. You want them to settle as soon as possible throughout the night feeds so make sure this feed isn't rushed. Wind well, change their nappy and offer a top-up.

Swaddle and put baby back to bed. This feed should take roughly an hour.

1 a.m. I find this the hardest feed to wake up for – but don't worry, have in mind that this feed is soon dropped.

Wake baby, feed, wind, change nappy, and offer a top-up.

It's really tempting to put baby back to bed if they are sleepy after half a feed, but motivate yourself to finish the full feed so that they are settled until the next feed and they don't wake you up in half an hour's time.

Swaddle and put baby back to bed. Use white noise if baby is struggling to fall asleep.

4 a.m. Wake baby, feed, wind, change nappy and offer a top-up. Swaddle and put baby back to bed. Use white noise if baby is struggling to fall asleep.

Week 1 Day 4

Something to remember is that bonding with your baby can sometimes take time, especially if you had a difficult birth. Be patient and enjoy plenty of cuddles and skin-to-skin with your little one. It will come.

FACT About a third of babies are born with a birthmark of some kind. The most common type is a stork mark, also known as a salmon patch. This pale pink patch, which may appear redder when your baby cries, usually disappears within six months. Most birthmarks are harmless and will disappear on their own but if your baby has a mark or other unexplained bumps or colouring on their skin, ask your midwife to have a look.

FOOD FOR THOUGHT It is advised that all breastfed babies take a Vitamin D supplement from birth. However, babies who are having more than 500ml (17fl oz) of formula a day don't need vitamin supplements because it's already in their formula.

TIP Buy babygrows with built-in mittens. Fold the mitten over your baby's hands while they sleep to keep them warm and cosy and to stop them scratching themselves. The most practical items to dress your newborn in are a vest, babygrow and cardigan. It keeps them snug and comfortable. Cotton vests and babygrows are easy to throw in the wash together, and cardigans can be taken off when baby is swaddled or during feeding to stop them getting too warm and sleepy. When dressing your baby, stretch the necks on the vests with your hands before putting them over babies' heads to create more room.

Week 1 Day 5

Now that your baby is almost two weeks old, you will start to notice they become more wakeful and engaged.

Some newborn babies prefer to turn their heads to one side rather than the other. This is called infant torticollis and can be due to positioning in the womb or a difficult birth. Observe your baby over the first few weeks when you put them on a changing mat, in their cot or even in the bath and work out which side their head naturally falls towards. If they always turn their head to the left, approach them in their cot from the right-hand side and talk to them so that they practise turning their head towards you.

FACT You may think your baby looks a bit cross-eyed for the first few weeks but as their eyes strengthen and open they should begin to focus. At first, newborns see mostly in black and white and can only focus up to about 20 cm away. Use a black felt tip and draw some images on white card, then prop them up next to your baby in the pram or by their changing mat. Babies love the contrast of black and white patterns and will often lie quietly looking at them. This can also encourage them to look both ways.

FOOD FOR THOUGHT I would advise getting into the habit of taking a daily postnatal supplement that includes essential nutrients such as iron, vitamin C, calcium and B12.

HOW TO Follow the link on this QR code to discover a great hack when dealing with explosive nappies!

Week 1 Day 6

The night feeds might be starting to get tough – remember that this isn't forever. Try not to rush night-time feeds and make sure your baby is winded really well before they go back down, so that they will sleep for a good chunk of time and not have you up again in half an hour due to hunger or discomfort.

FOOD FOR THOUGHT Try making my Oat Bites. Oats not only support lactation, but they also provide slow-release energy. They are easy to make and can be frozen in batches.

Ingredients

2–3 ripe bananas
60g porridge oats
30g apple sauce
1 teaspoon ground cinnamon

1. Preheat the oven to 180°C.
2. Mash the bananas with the back of a fork in a bowl.
3. Add the oats, apple sauce and ground cinnamon and mix well.
4. Divide into 10 balls and put on a baking tray lined with baking paper. Bake for 15–20 minutes or until golden.
5. Remove and leave to cool on a wire rack.

TIP These bites only stay fresh for two days but are suitable for freezing, so wrap them individually in baking paper and pop in a bag in the freezer. You can then take them out in the morning and use them for snacks; they only take a couple of hours to defrost.

2 Weeks Old

Wow – two weeks old already!

FACT Your baby's tummy has grown to the size of a hen's egg.

FOOD FOR THOUGHT Babies and older children go through periods of growth spurts. It is very possible your little one is having a growth spurt if they are sleeping for longer, hungrier and . . . growing!

Your breastfed baby may feed for longer and a bottle-fed baby might not be satisfied after their usual amount of milk, so top up with an extra 30–60 ml (1–2 fl oz).

Growth spurts can happen at any time but often occur at roughly two weeks; three weeks; six weeks; three months; four months; five months; six months and nine months.

The growth spurts will last for a few days so let your baby have a little extra sleep at their morning nap if they need it, and go with their increased appetite.

MINDFULNESS Today, try to enjoy a peaceful shower while your baby is napping. Switch on the shower and focus on the feeling of the water on your skin. Consider what the temperature feels like, question how you actually know if it's hot or cold, reflect on how it feels. Before using a shower gel or face wash, smell the product and be in the moment. Your mindfulness matters.

Week 2 Day 1

FACT After the first two weeks, breastfed babies can go for up to six days without pooing. This is because their body needs to take every nutrient from the milk.

FOOD FOR THOUGHT: Red meat will help boost your iron levels. Try my Spaghetti Bolognese recipe, which you can freeze in smaller batches or let the whole family enjoy! This recipe serves six.

Ingredients

3 rashers of streaky bacon or pancetta
2 onions, chopped
4 garlic cloves, crushed
3 carrots, peeled and chopped
2 sticks of celery, chopped
1 red pepper, cored and diced
2 tablespoons olive oil
600g beef mince
2 × 400g tin chopped tomatoes
2 tablespoons tomato purée
500ml beef stock
3 fresh bay leaves
6 button mushrooms, sliced
8 cherry tomatoes, halved
500g dried spaghetti pasta

1. In a large pan, sauté the bacon, onion, garlic, carrot, celery and red pepper on a low heat with the olive oil until softened.
2. Stir in the beef, turn the heat up and cook for 5–10 minutes, until the meat is browned all over.
3. Add the tinned tomatoes, tomato purée, stock and bay leaves. Stir well, turning the heat up to bring to the boil.
4. Reduce to a low heat, then cover and simmer for around 1 hour, stirring occasionally.
5. Remove the lid, take the three bay leaves out and add the mushrooms and cherry tomatoes. Continue cooking for 20 minutes, to thicken and reduce. Meanwhile, in another pan, cook the spaghetti pasta according to the packet instructions.
6. Drain the pasta when cooked and serve with the Bolognese.

Week 2 Day 2

It is common for newborns to get a cold or be a bit snuffly this week, but please don't worry. Here are some tips to help:

- Use a saline spray and nose sucker regularly throughout the day to help clear their nose, especially before a feed.
- Use a humidifier in their room while sleeping.
- Blocked noses become worse at night so help your baby sleep by raising the top end of their cot using books under the legs, so that they sleep on a slight incline.

TIP Each evening, before you go to bed, get everything ready for the night feeds so that you aren't stumbling around in the dark during the night. Make sure you have a supply of bibs, muslins, nappies, wipes and spare clothes in case your baby is sick or pees over his pyjamas.

A night feed is slightly different to a feed in the day because you want baby to stay in a sleepy mode so that they settle quickly after being fed. There isn't as much eye contact or talking to your baby at night, but they still need a proper feed, changing and winding throughout the feeding period.

I find a nightlight very useful if you haven't got dimmer lights. You can also use the torch light on your phone instead of putting a main light on.

FACT As many as 80 per cent of women may experience the baby blues – feeling low, tired and tearful – within the first few weeks of parenthood. It's totally normal. Don't hesitate to reach out to your midwife, health visitor or GP for support.

Week 2 Day 3

FACT Hiccups are very common in newborns and are nothing to worry about. Some babies are more prone to them than others and you will find that some babies even hiccup regularly in the womb. Hiccups are caused by sudden contractions of the diaphragm and usually happen just after a feed, or when your baby gets excited or laughs. To help ease hiccups you can continue to feed your baby by breast or bottle to ease them away, or offer a few sips of cooled boiled water out of a bottle if it isn't occurring during a feed.

FOOD FOR THOUGHT To help your milk supply, enjoy this Breastfeeding Smoothie today – it contains three key lactation-boosting ingredients: flaxseed, oats and brewer's yeast.

Ingredients
1 frozen banana
8 strawberries
1 teaspoon brewer's yeast
2 tablespoons oats
1 teaspoon flaxseed
1 teaspoon honey
Milk – add enough to get your preferred consistency.

Simply blitz and serve.

ACTIVITY Use an ink pad or paint to capture your baby's footprints. They make a lovely keepsake for you to treasure, and can also be used to make cards for family and friends. One day you won't believe how tiny they were!

Bring the card or paper to your baby's toes, rather than trying to put their feet on the paper.

Write this little poem below their footprints to make a beautiful keepsake or gift:

This is to remind you
When I have grown so tall
That once I was quite little
And my feet were very small

Don't forget to make an extra one to put in your memory box!

Week 2 Day 4

Today is a good time to start some gentle pelvic floor exercises.

Practise this simple exercise for a few minutes each day, or twice a day if you can remember. I promise you'll thank me for it later!

HOW TO Take a deep breath in. As you exhale, imagine you're trying to stop wind from your back passage and then keep trying to draw your anus up. Hold for up to 10 seconds: you may only be able to hold it for a second or two at the beginning so work on keeping it up for longer each day. You'll know your pelvic floor muscles are getting stronger when you can hold for longer.

As you exhale, let your pelvic floor fully relax. The relaxing of the pelvic floor is just as important as the contracting.

TIP It is common for newborns to experience sticky eyes due to blocked tearducts. Using cooled boiled water on a cotton pad, wipe their eyes from the inside out to keep them clean at each feed.

Week 2 Day 5

Listening to a favourite piece of music releases feel-good endorphins. Playing classical music creates a calming atmosphere for the whole family to enjoy, and also aids your baby's cognitive development. When they listen to classical music it stimulates their brain, improving their IQ, creativity, mood and hearing.

FOOD FOR THOUGHT People have so many opinions about the way you feed your baby. I never want you to feel pressured – do what is right for you and your baby. You won't be able to tell the difference later down the line whether a child was breastfed or bottle fed; it's more important that you and your baby are relaxed and happy.

ACTIVITY Make a playlist for your little one and listen to it together. Add a new song every day and by the time they turn one you will have a vast collection. Listening to the songs will always remind you of this special time.

Play music from a device or your phone while you are changing their nappy or when they are having a kick on their playmat.

Week 2 Day 6

You may find that by this point, you are feeling quite tired. Don't worry, this is completely normal and to be expected.

It's really important to catch up on lost sleep during the day. Even half an hour will make a difference. Here are some more tips:

- Drink lots of water and try to get a bit of fresh air at least once a day. No matter how tired you feel, if you get out – even to sit in the garden – it will make you feel much better.
- A facial mist is refreshing, wakes you up and hydrates your skin. A couple of sprays on your face will help you come around from your sleep!
- Roll-on eye gel is cooling on your skin and helps those eye bags! Apply before going to sleep after each feed and when you wake.
- Netflix! Find a good series and feed time won't drag. It helps you stay awake and stops you clock-watching while your little one feeds – just keep the glare and volume low.
- Use a water bottle with a straw, lots of ice and a natural flavour, such as apple, mint, lemon or cucumber. I find being up in the night can make you thirsty, especially if you are breastfeeding.
- Snacks: breastfeeding mums get really hungry in the night so take some snacks to bed with you. Popular snacks when feeding include flapjacks, dried apricots, oatcakes, digestive biscuits, malt loaf, banana, fig rolls and satsumas.

I know it's hard when you are sleep-deprived, but don't be in such a rush to put baby down that they haven't finished a proper feed or been winded enough. In the long run, it will only delay you as they won't settle or will wake early for their next feed.

After a feed, once baby is changed and hasn't got any wind, spend a couple of minutes with your little one on your chest to relax them and make them feel secure. Then swaddle them and put them back down.

3 Weeks Old

FACT Baby acne – or milk spots as I like to call them – are spots that appear on a baby's face at about three weeks old. They are thought to be due to a combination of the hormones in your baby's body and the pores opening up on delicate baby skin. You can help prevent the spots by keeping baby's face clean and dry so that grease and dirt doesn't build up.

HOW TO Top and tailing in the morning and evening is the best remedy for clogged skin. Watch my top and tailing video to learn how.

ACTIVITY Learn this little rhyme which you can sing to your baby. Hearing your voice and a repetitive tune will bring them so much joy.

Such little fingers and such tiny toes
Such lively eyes and such an adorable nose
A mouth so tiny and a smile so sweet
You are the cutest little baby I ever did meet

Week 3 Day 1

Have you thought about weighing your baby? It's a way to make sure your little one is feeding well and putting on weight steadily each week. Some weeks your baby will put on more weight than others, but you will hopefully see a gradual increase. Record their weekly weights in their red book (your personal child health record book, which you should have been given by your health visitor or midwife). Ideally, you should weigh your baby at the same time of day – decide whether this is before or after a feed so your readings are consistent. I tend to weigh babies once a week before their bathtime, as they are already undressed. You can buy baby weighing scales, or you can stand on adult scales with your baby and deduct your weight to get their reading.

FACT Babies don't cry tears in the first month. Their tear ducts can only produce enough tears to protect and coat the eye but not enough for a tear to roll down their cheek.

TIP Try eating earlier at 5 p.m. That way, once baby is settled at 7.30 p.m. you don't have to worry about starting to cook again, and it means you can have a bath and get a few hours' sleep in before the late feed. Lots of parents have said this makes a huge difference to their day in the first few newborn weeks.

Week 3 Day 2

As you read this, think how lucky you are to have your baby with you. Think of one thing you are grateful for today.

As a parent, there will always be moments when you feel overwhelmed, guilty or anxious – that's normal, and I'm pretty confident that *every* parent has felt these emotions. You are often doing several tasks at once, while also thinking about a hundred other things. By practising mindfulness and focusing your mind on one thing at a time, it brings you to the present and detaches you from all the other elements of stress. Mindfulness is something you can practise anywhere at any time.

ACTIVITY If you have any black-and-white patterned muslins, drape one over the side of baby's Moses basket and let your little one have a stretch and a kick while looking at the bold design.

MINDFULNESS Take a moment today to sit with your baby in your arms and really observe their features: look at their ears, their toes, their fingers and their nose. Take a deep breath, smile at them, and tell them what it is that you adore about them. I would love you to take just a few minutes every day to have this uninterrupted moment with your little one.

Week 3 Day 3

From today, start to incorporate some daily tummy time into your baby's routine.

There are many benefits to tummy time:

- It helps build up the strength needed in your baby's back, neck and shoulder muscles for future rolling and crawling.
- It gets your baby familiar with being on their front so that crawling isn't daunting.
- Because babies have to sleep on their backs, it relieves pressure from the back of their heads for a few moments each day.
- It means they don't have to look at bright ceiling lights when they're playing.
- It can help babies who are experiencing a sore tummy by putting a little pressure on the area. The new position can also sometimes move niggly gas through the digestive system.
- A new position with some interesting things to look at and explore is stimulating for a baby and stops them getting bored. They can start to reach for toys and use cognitive skills different from those used when they are on their backs.
- It's a good way for you to see their full body, to see any changes in their head shape (see page 80) and keep an eye on all their movements to make sure each limb is stretching and moving equally.

To give your baby tummy time, roll up a blanket or towel and place your little one onto a comfortable surface with their upper body and arms draped over the rolled-up material to help support them. By giving this added support they will enjoy tummy time for longer.

Only put your baby in this position for a few minutes at a time – it is very tiring for them and takes up a lot of energy and strength! Talk to them while they are on their front, giving them the reassurance and confidence that you are still there. Never leave your little one; supervise them at all times while they are on their tummy.

At first, only lay them there for less than a minute each time, but as your baby's neck muscles strengthen they will enjoy this activity for longer.

Build tummy time into your everyday routine. A good time to practise it is in the morning when they are getting dressed, and in the evenings before bathtime. If they look like they're not enjoying it, gently turn them onto their back and tell them how clever they are, then try again tomorrow.

Week 3 Day 4

Today I want to talk to you about sleep, as I'm sure it's something you are wanting a bit more of. A baby's night will reflect their day, so if they have good naps during the day they will sleep better at night.

Understanding your baby's sleep cycles will explain why sometimes you could play a trumpet and your sleeping baby won't stir, and other times simply walking past their Moses basket wakes them. This is because they are in either a deep or REM sleep.

When falling asleep we go into a light sleep, then into a deep one, then we go into an even deeper sleep, before coming out into a deep, and then light sleep again. The light sleep stage is called REM (rapid eye movement). This is when your baby is much more likely to wake. During REM sleep you might see your baby's eyelids moving or fluttering.

A baby's complete sleep cycle is roughly forty minutes, but this gets longer as we move through childhood and into adulthood. If your baby is disturbed by noise, feels cold, is hungry, rouses in a different place to the one they fell asleep in, or doesn't feel secure, then they will wake during REM sleep rather than linking their sleep cycles. So don't assume that if your baby wakes after a short nap, they have had enough sleep.

Learning to be a good sleeper can take time, patience, the continuity of a daily routine and a happy sleeping space.

I believe that your baby will sleep more soundly at night if they experience fresh air during the day. Taking this into consideration, I would encourage your little one to have at least one of their naps outdoors in the fresh air.

FACT Babies are naturally nocturnal. This means we have to wake them for regular feeds throughout the day and offer them periods of stimulation during daylight hours so that they settle quickly during the night-time, rather than want to party at night!

Week 3 Day 5

Today I want you to think about something that will help your feeding journey further down the line: how to prevent bottle refusal.

After a few weeks, once breastfeeding is established, I recommend giving your baby one bottle a day. At this early stage, babies are happy to go from breast to bottle and it gets them used to the feeling of having a teat in their mouth. I recommend doing this so that if your baby is weaned on to the bottle, there won't be any fuss or distress for them.

I have had a couple of families who have solely breastfed for several months and then Mum has had to go into hospital unexpectedly. In these cases, the baby has been very distressed and refused to take a bottle, which is traumatic for everyone. If you plan to return to work, it is also a good idea to introduce the bottle once a day from early on.

I suggest this one bottle feed as a 'top-up' feed in the evenings, after bathtime. It's also a great opportunity for your partner to feed your baby, which is good for their bonding as well as giving you a break!

Depending on how much milk you have, how you are feeling and how hungry your baby is, you can:

- Express milk and give it to them in a bottle.
- Express and store this milk and give your baby formula for this one feed.
- Express and mix the breastmilk with formula.

The important thing is to offer one of these 'top-up' feeds daily to avoid bottle refusal later.

Week 3 Day 6

You might have noticed that your baby is managing to stay awake for longer periods of time now and is starting to observe the world around them more.

If you haven't already, I would encourage you to buy a play gym for your baby. Play gyms are a stimulating space for your baby to lie, kick, wriggle and explore!

After their morning feed, they can enjoy some nappy-free time on their mat before getting dressed. Put a towel or disposable changing mat under them to catch any accidents. You can also let them enjoy their mat before they have a bath in the evening. The reason I take their nappy off is to let their skin breathe (which helps to prevent nappy rash) and allow them freedom to move their legs without being restricted.

Interacting with their play gym will improve your baby's cognitive skills. The toys overhead will aid their visual perspective and encourage them to grasp objects and practise their grip strength.

ACTIVITY Three ways to use your play gym:

1. Hang black-and-white patterned muslins to the arches.
2. Let your baby practise tummy time while on the mat.
3. Prop black and white images against the frame of the play gym for your baby to look at.

4 Weeks Old

ACTIVITY Document your baby's growth with the help of a teddy bear positioned alongside them.

Lay your little one alongside a favourite teddy bear and take a photograph. I will remind you to repeat this once a month so that by their first birthday, you will have twelve photographs to keep. By using the same teddy bear each month, you will get a perspective on how much they have grown and you'll wonder how it was possible that they changed so much in 365 days!

MINDFULNESS Sit on a chair with your back straight and your feet flat on the floor. Take some long, slow breaths and focus on the feeling of your feet. Wriggle your toes then place them flat again. Scratch the top of your head and concentrate on the feeling it gives you. Relax your shoulders as you continue to take slow, deep breaths.

Week 4 Day 1

Let's talk about crying . . .

Crying is one of the main ways a newborn expresses and communicates their needs to us. Every baby is different and some verbalise through crying more than others. All babies have different cries, too. Some are quiet, whereas others are piercingly loud!

Observe your baby when they cry to see if they are just a bit cross and having what I call a 'shout', or if they are distressed or in discomfort. Some babies like to have a bit of a grumble before they go to sleep; it's their settling method.

When your baby cries it could be due to a number of reasons. Try to put yourself in their position and see if they could be:

- **Overtired**
  This is often overlooked – and a tired baby can be very fractious. If your baby is crying because they're overtired, swaddle them and tuck them into their cot or pram. They might continue to cry for a few minutes but will settle quicker than if they are kept up or cuddled to stop the crying and then put down.
- **Hungry**
  If your baby finds it hard to go to sleep and then wakes after short periods, and cries a lot between feeds, they probably aren't getting enough milk to be satisfied. Try longer feeds if you are breastfeeding, or offer more milk in a bottle.
- **Suffering from trapped wind**
  This is painful and uncomfortable for a baby. Make sure you wind your baby during and after each feed to prevent a build-up of gas.

- **Cold**
  Babies can't move around enough to keep warm so make sure they are well wrapped up outside. I also find a lot of babies aren't kept warm enough at night, which can wake them and cause them to cry.
- **Too hot**
  If baby's face is red or they are sweating on their neck or back, they are too hot. Car seats can get incredibly hot so take coats off and then layer with a blanket on the top, which you can take off easily if necessary. If you have a plastic rain cover on the pram, remember it can have the effect of creating a little greenhouse under the cover. Take it off when not needed or open the vents for air to get into the pram.

There is no doubt that listening to a crying baby can make anyone anxious and sometimes stressed, especially when the baby is your responsibility and you are sleep-deprived. If you ever feel overwhelmed, or like you are losing control of your anger, put your baby in their cot and walk away for a few minutes to calm down.

Week 4 Day 2

You have been caring for your baby for a whole month now and it's time to think of yourself today. You must realise that taking care of yourself is part of taking care of your baby.

Here are a few examples of how you can practise self-care:

- Book a blow dry
- Have a manicure
- Relax in a daytime bath
- Enjoy a guilt-free nap
- Meet a friend for coffee

A happy parent makes a happy baby.

ACTIVITY Take a walk with your baby while they enjoy the motion of the pram and hopefully have a sleep. Research shows that breathing in fresh air relieves stress, clears the mind and reduces anxiety.

Week 4 Day 3

FOOD FOR THOUGHT Why not try making my Overnight Oats Breakfast Inspiration? You can make this tasty breakfast up to three days before you eat it, so it's brilliant for having on hand after a long night. Oats provide slow-release energy and will help support your breastmilk production.

Simply combine oats with any type of milk – cow's, almond, soya, oat, chocolate – in a jar or container, using enough milk to cover the oats. Mix well before adding in any other flavourings. Cover and leave to soak in the fridge overnight. The oats are delicious served cold, or heated and served warm.

My two favourite flavours are:

- Chia seeds and honey – add a sprinkling of chia seeds and squeeze of honey into the oats and milk before leaving to soak.
- Peanut butter – add a dollop of peanut butter into the oats and milk and mix together before soaking.

ACTIVITY Write a dated letter to your baby which you can add to their memory box. Write about how they have changed, where you have been and the people they have met.

Week 4 Day 4

Using a white noise in the room that your baby sleeps in will help them settle more easily and will become their sleep cue. It blocks out external noise, helping your little one to link their sleep cycles. If you live in a noisy household with older siblings or live by a busy road, for instance, white noise helps to drown out sounds that could disturb your baby. There are white noise machines available to buy that you can put in your baby's room and leave them playing all night, or you can simply use your phone to play a waterfall noise for twenty minutes to help your baby fall asleep.

FACT Although your little one can hear well, their middle ear is still full of fluid, which will impair their hearing until they get a bit older. This is why your baby will respond to you more if you use a high-pitched and exaggerated tone of voice.

FOOD FOR THOUGHT If your baby is gaining weight and feeding regularly throughout the day, start to let them stretch longer at night-time so that their body clock adjusts to being hungrier during the day than they are during the night. This will set you on the path for great night-time sleeping.

Stick to the daily routine by starting their day at 7 a.m. and continue to follow the feeding times shown in the routine.

TIP If you had a C-section and your scar is aching, put a cold compress on the area to ease the pain.

Week 4 Day 5

In the first stages of breastfeeding while your baby learns to latch on, you may find it easier to feed in the comfort of your own home, but once you feel more confident try feeding when you are out and about. Think about what you're wearing before you leave the house: choose your preferred feeding top and nursing bra. I advise you wear a loose vest top under a jumper, so you can pull the jumper up and the vest top down to create a peep hole without revealing too much skin.

Try to plan where you will be when it's time to feed. You might want to find a café or a park bench. It might be helpful to take your partner, friend or a relative with you for the first couple of times, especially if you have other children with you. They can be an extra pair of hands and can look after the older ones while you feed!

Don't hide in a loo to feed; it's dirty and depressing for you. It's perfectly fine for you to feed in any public place – cafés, restaurants, in the playground, etc. Many department stores and shopping centres have designated feeding rooms so you could check these ahead of your trip.

If you are nervous about feeding in public, practise at home in front of a mirror. You will be surprised at how little is exposed. If you still feel self-conscious, you could use a feeding cover (a large muslin tied around your neck works just as well), which you can keep in your baby bag.

FACT Babies have no kneecaps when they are born . . . instead they have cartilage that looks like a kneecap. Kneecaps do not develop until they are approximately six months old.

Week 4 Day 6

'Eat when the baby eats' is a good phrase to remember while you are feeding and will help boost your energy levels.

FACT Your body can burn up to 500 calories per day when breastfeeding, so it's really important for you and your baby that you eat well and often.

FOOD FOR THOUGHT Foods such as butternut squash, chia seeds, lean meat, pulses, nuts and seeds are recommended as they are filling and nutritious. Eating healthy foods will also help you feel energised and better mentally.

One of my favourite recipes is this Red Lentil Soup. It's super easy to make and packed with 'good for you' ingredients. Batch-cook a big saucepan of this and freeze in smaller portions, so that you always have a nutritious lunch waiting for you. This recipe serves four.

Ingredients
1 onion, chopped
1 bag of carrots, peeled and roughly chopped
2–3 leeks, roughly chopped
1 celery stalk, chopped
Butter or oil
250g red lentils
500 ml chicken or vegetable stock

1. In a large pan, sweat the onion, carrots, leeks and celery for 10 minutes in butter or oil until soft.
2. Add the red lentils and enough stock to generously cover all the vegetables, and cook for a further 10 minutes.
3. Blitz until smooth and add seasoning if required.

5 Weeks Old

I only want you to do one thing today.

Please follow the link on this QR code to watch this video on baby CPR (a life-saving resuscitation technique that you would use in the event that your little one stops breathing). Hopefully you will never ever have to use this, but if you do, you will have the skills.

Please share this with any of your friends who have a baby under twelve months old.

Week 5 Day 1

If your baby is taking 120ml (4fl oz) per feed now, they might be ready to move on to Routine 2 – see pages 59 to 61. If you are breastfeeding, try expressing one of your feeds so that you know the quantity that your little one is getting – it's always really useful to know.

Your baby needs to be naturally stretching for longer periods between feeds at night before you implement the four-hourly routine during the day – we always want their longer periods of sleep to be at night-time.

Signs that your little one is ready to move on to Routine 2:

- They weigh over 3.6kg (8lbs+).
- They are not hungry after three hours or they will only have a snack rather than a big feed.
- They consistently drink 120ml+ (4fl oz+) at each feed.

FOOD FOR THOUGHT You want to continuously have in your mind that your baby should be upping their milk quantity as they grow each week. This will enable them to have longer breaks between feeds.

TIP Always offer your baby a top-up feed. Think of it as the second part of the feed, like a pudding. When we eat, we often enjoy most of our main meal, then slow down and take a little break before finishing the last bit. This is the same for babies. They will take a large amount of milk, then after a break for winding and to have a nappy change, you'll often find they have room for a top-up. Your baby's feed shouldn't last more than an hour, so offer the top-up within an hour of starting the feed. Offering this top-up will help your baby stretch and work towards Routine 2.

Routine 2

0 to 3 Months: The Four-Hourly Cycle

If your baby weighs over 3.6kg (8lbs), they may be happy to feed every four hours after a week or so of feeding every three hours, especially through the night. Bottle-fed babies tend to fall into this routine a little quicker than breastfed babies. On the four-hourly routine, baby will feed six times per twenty-four hours, so their tummies need to be able to take at least 120ml (4fl oz) at each feed.

If your baby doesn't settle after a feed, try picking them up in their swaddle and winding them on your shoulder. If they are rooting (bobbing their head trying to find more food) or sucking on their fingers, they are probably still hungry. When they have relaxed and aren't crying or squirming, put them back in their bed and tuck them in with a blanket over the top so that baby feels snug and secure. Use white noise to see if baby can settle.

7 a.m. Wake, feed, wind. Change nappy, have some nappy-free time (if the umbilical cord has fallen off), top and tail, moisturise and dress baby for the day. Offer a top-up.

8.45 a.m. Swaddle and put down for a nap. This is a lovely time for a sleep in the pram outside.

11 a.m. Wake baby, feed, wind, change nappy. Offer a top-up. Aim to have baby awake for roughly two hours, so if they woke at 10.30 a.m. then they will be ready for bed at 12.30 p.m., but if you had to wake them at 11 a.m. then they may be able to stretch until 1 p.m. for their next nap.

3 p.m. Wake baby, feed, wind, nappy change, offer a top-up.

4 p.m. A shorter nap of up to an hour.

5 p.m. Wake baby for some awake time.

5.45 p.m. Start bathtime. Offer a split feed* if needed.

6.15 p.m. Big feed and lots of time winding.

7 p.m. Swaddle and put baby to bed.

11 p.m. Wake baby: turn on the lights to make sure they wake properly and have a really good feed. Wind and change nappy. Offer a top-up feed. Swaddle and put back to bed.

3 a.m. Wake, feed, wind, change nappy. Offer a top-up. Swaddle and put back to bed. Use white noise if baby is struggling to fall back asleep.

Note: Once your baby has established a good four-hourly routine, the first feed that you want to drop is either the 11 p.m. or the 3 a.m. feed. This is usually at around eight weeks old.

You have two options:

1) Put baby to bed at 7 p.m. and let them sleep for as long as they can without waking them. They usually wake at around 1 a.m. to begin with. Give them a big feed when they wake so they can get as close to the morning feed as possible. They will sometimes wake at 5 or 6 a.m.; if they do, offer a small feed and tuck them back into bed for another sleep before you start the day at 7 a.m.

   The benefit of this is that you can go to bed early and don't have to wait up to do the last feed. Tip: if you have older children, eat with them at teatime so that once everyone is in

---

* The 'split feed': at bathtime, if your baby isn't enjoying their bath because they're hungry, offer them half a feed before their bath and the other half afterwards. After a few weeks, your baby should be happy to relax and enjoy their bath before having their bedtime feed. Don't bath a baby after a full feed as it will often cause them to be sick.

bed you can go to sleep and not have to worry about preparing another meal. This often gives you a longer stretch of sleep. I always do this and I find it helps so much.

2) Or: wake baby for a 'dream feed' at 11 p.m. and then leave them to sleep and see if they can stretch until 6.30 a.m. If baby wakes before 6 a.m., do the same as above; offer a small feed and tuck them back into bed for a sleep before you start the day at 7 a.m.

Continuing the dream feed at 11 p.m. or letting them have their longer stretch of sleep in the evening is a personal preference. I have done it both ways. Personally, I find letting them stretch as far as they can after bedtime makes it easier for babies to get to 7 a.m. the next morning without having a second feed. But discuss it with your partner as you may strike a deal: if they stay up and feed baby at 11 p.m., letting you go to bed early . . . you could be sleeping for a whole night!

Week 5 Day 2

Are you finding the hardest time to wake up is in the morning at 7 a.m. when your body says it would like a few more hours of sleep? I know it's tempting to wait until your baby wakes you up to get those extra few minutes in bed but I always find it more beneficial to set your alarm fifteen minutes before baby is due his feed, get yourself up, then have some water or a cup of tea and a shower before your baby wakes. It's amazing how much more awake you feel after a shower and then you are ready to start the day with your family. If you are dressed and feel half-human before your little one is awake, I promise your day will go more smoothly!

FOOD FOR THOUGHT Try my Banana Bread recipe for a delicious snack, which will also boost your energy levels. Bananas are good to include in your diet, especially while breastfeeding, as they contain vitamins such as vitamin B, folate and vitamin C, which are good for both you and your baby.

Ingredients
140g caster sugar
140g softened butter
2 eggs
140g self-raising flour
2 ripe bananas

1. Preheat the oven to 180°C and line a loaf tin with greaseproof paper.
2. In a mixing bowl, cream the sugar and softened butter together until it is pale and fluffy.
3. Add the eggs and beat in until they are well combined.
4. Sift and fold in the flour.
5. Mash the bananas and add to the bowl. Stir in gently then pour the mixture into the loaf tin.
6. Bake for 20–25 minutes or until golden brown.

Week 5 Day 3

If you are bottle feeding, your periods may return in the next few weeks. They can often be irregular to begin with. After a few cycles they should start to settle back into a regular pattern again.

Your first period post-birth may feel different to the ones you were experiencing before pregnancy. You may have heavier bleeding and more intense cramping. Again, don't worry as this is usually normal. However, if you pass blood clots or are struggling to keep on top of heavy bleeding then speak to your GP.

FACT It's a myth that you can't get pregnant while breastfeeding. You can get pregnant as soon as twenty-one days after giving birth, so remember to think about contraception unless you want to get pregnant again quickly.

ACTIVITY Listen to a piece of your favourite music with your baby. Choose a time today when your baby is fed and winded and hold them up on your shoulder while you sway with them as you listen to the song. Drink in their smell and enjoy the moment. Your baby might like it if you hum a little tune in their ear.

Week 5 Day 4

If you are breastfeeding, you may experience cracked nipples. This can occur if your baby isn't latching on properly. You may notice some blood in your milk but this isn't harmful to your baby and you can continue to breastfeed.

TIP To prevent cracked nipples, make sure your baby is latched on and in a good position for feeding. If feeding is painful, or you feel baby slipping off, remove them by gently inserting your little finger into the corner of your baby's mouth to break the seal, and try latching them on again. After each feed, rub some breast milk onto your nipples and let them air dry before putting your bra back on. Use a nipple cream, change your breast pads frequently and use warm flannels to help ease the pain. Silver nursing cups are brilliant for helping with cracked nipples and sit inside your bra between feeds.

ACTIVITY Get into the habit of saying a cheery good morning to your baby before you pick them up out of their cot in the morning. They will hear your voice and not be startled when you pick them up. If they respond to your voice by turning their head to look at you, stand over their Moses basket or cot and have a chat with them before taking their swaddle off. I always think it's a way of helping them to feel happy and secure in their bed and in their own space and it's a lovely, positive way to start each morning.

FACT Your baby's head makes up a quarter of their total body length right now.

Week 5 Day 5

Today is all about poo, sorry!

Your child's poo can tell you a lot about what is going on inside their bodies – especially with a newborn, who can't communicate verbally to tell you if their tummy is hurting. That's why it's important to know what's normal and what's not.

Poo will differ depending on whether your baby is breastfed or formula-fed. Breastfed poos will differ in colour depending on what you have eaten, whereas formula poo tends to be more consistent in colour – although it can still vary.

Breastfed babies' poo may look like it contains seeds. This is undigested milk fat and totally normal. Formula poo has a pastier consistency, almost like peanut butter!

Babies can strain and go red in the face when they are trying to poo, even if the poo is soft when it comes out. This is normal, but if your baby is consistently unhappy (bringing legs up, crying, hard tummy) when they poo, consult your GP.

FACT Unbelievably, you will change around 2,000 nappies this year!

TIP If you feel that your little one is trying to poo without any luck, move their legs in a cycling motion while they are lying on a changing mat. The rhythm of this movement can often get things moving.

Week 5 Day 6

At some point in the next two weeks, you should have your postnatal check with your GP. Your baby will also have their six-to-eight-week check at around the same time. This is to ensure you are both healthy and that you are recovering well from the birth. This is a good opportunity to discuss any concerns you may have.

TIP Write a list of questions before you go to your appointment, so you don't forget to ask any burning questions once there.

ACTIVITY Today, create a folder to keep all your baby's important documents inside and find a safe place so that you always know where to reach them in a hurry. Write their name and NHS number on the front.

Things to include in your baby's folder:

- Their red book (your personal child health record book)
- Passport
- Birth certificate
- Health visitor notes

6 Weeks Old

Exercise is a great way of doing something for yourself, releasing feel-good endorphins and helping you to feel physically stronger.

If you have had a straightforward vaginal birth you can think about gently returning to exercise now, if you have had the sign off from your doctor and everything feels OK.

Remember to start slowly. Your body has been through a lot and your organs have moved gradually over the course of nine months so they will take time to resettle. Keep it low impact and use light weights to start.

Avoid doing things like sit-ups and straight leg raises for a while. Cat/cow stretches are an ideal physical activity to gently ease you back into exercise.

HOW TO To do a cat/cow stretch, kneel on your hands and knees. Breathing is key here! Take a deep breath in, let your tummy and chest expand, drop your back down and let your head tilt back.

As you exhale a long, deep breath out through your mouth (like you're blowing out a candle), arch your back up, drop your head down and draw your tummy in as much as possible to try to make your waist very small. This will work your deep abdominal muscles.

FACT Your uterus can take up to ten weeks to shrink back to its original size, so don't worry if your belly looks bloated for a few months after birth.

Week 6 Day 1

Today I want to introduce you to baby massage! This is a wonderful bonding experience for you and your baby and one that has many benefits. I use baby massage after bathtime as a nightly routine. Your little one will love the feeling of your touch and it draws out their bedtime hour when they might be tired and looking for their bedtime milk.

Massage is really beneficial for your baby's circulation and also helps settle them into their bedtime routine. Massage can help aid sleep, teething pain and digestion. It's also a lovely bonding time for partners who aren't able to feed, as well as mums who can.

You will need a cream or oil. I like to use coconut oil as it's a natural moisturising product and babies go to bed smelling as sweet as little coconuts.

Make the room warm and cosy, and find a comfortable position for you and your baby. You might want to lie them on a bed in front of you with a soft towel around them, or you might find it easier on their changing mat. Make sure your baby isn't looking up at any blinding lights.

Some safety notes:

- Don't use peanut-based oils in case it causes an allergic reaction.
- Do not attempt baby massage before six weeks old as newborns don't have enough meat on their bodies before then.
- It's also good to wait until after their six-week check to make sure there are no issues with hip dysplasia.

Follow the link on this QR code to see a video demonstrating how to do my bedtime massage.

Week 6 Day 2

Today think about creating a medicine box for your baby. Unfortunately, it is something that you will need to use at some point. During their childhood, when they do become poorly, symptoms often appear during the night. You will be relieved to have everything to hand and not have to worry about leaving the house to get these essentials.

Keep their medicine box in a high place that is out of reach of children.

The essential products to keep in your baby's medicine box are:

- Baby paracetamol
- Baby ibuprofen
- Digital thermometer
- Teething granules
- Nasal decongestant
- Baby nasal spray
- Sterile eye wash
- Antiseptic wipes
- Baby rehydration sachets
- Baby-friendly decongestant oil

TIP It's good practice to take your baby's temperature in both ears when they are well, to discover what their natural body temperature is. Every baby's natural body temperature sits slightly differently, although the average is 36.4 degrees Celsius. If you know what is normal for your baby, you will know when they are poorly if their temperature is raised.

Week 6 Day 3

Smiling is the first expression your baby will learn. It's a wonderful milestone and the first time you truly interact with each other. Your baby may have already given you some smiles, or they might be imminent. How do you tell the difference between a real smile and a windy one?

When your baby smiles due to having wind, it will occur randomly and they will often have their eyes closed. A real smile happens when your baby is responding to your voice or facial expressions. You will notice that their whole face lights up and their eyes smile at you as well as their mouth.

How to encourage those first smiles:

- Hold your baby in front of you and speak to them face to face at a time when they are comfortable and not hungry or tired.
- Use different tones while speaking to them.
- The more you smile, the more they will try to mimic your facial expression.
- Put them in a baby chair so they can see your whole face when you are talking to them. Remember to be within 30 cm of their face so they can see you clearly.
- Sing to them.
- Make different noises.
- Animate your voice while telling them how clever they are.
- Bathtime is another great time where babies often relax and follow the sound of your voice. If you talk to them you'll often get some smiles in the bath.
- I often prop little ones up on a pillow so they are elevated, supported and comfortable so they can concentrate on you and what you are saying to them.

FACT It's a myth that babies can't smile before they are six weeks old.

Week 6 Day 4

Let's talk about the importance of observation.

I want you to get to know what is the norm for your baby and their body. Observing them for just a few minutes each day means you can quickly pick up on any potential issues before they become a problem.

Watch your baby while they have just a nappy or vest on, or even better, without a nappy. I find that before bathtime or when you get them dressed in the morning are good times in the day to do a little body check. Make sure they aren't hungry or due a feed and that the room is warm enough for them to be comfortable. Look for any unusual marks that have appeared on their skin.

Lay your baby on their changing mat or on a comfortable and safe surface like your bed, and watch them while they kick and move their arms, checking they are moving all their limbs easily.

ACTIVITY Talk and smile to them while observing: play peekaboo, make different sounds, show them a toy – all while noting how they move. This should be a nice, relaxed activity, nothing that makes them think you're watching them. You're just interacting together!

FACT Babies are often sensitive to laundry detergent, so I advise using a non-biological one. Signs of skin irritation include dry, red and/or blotchy skin. Pay particular attention to the crooks of their arms and behind their knees.

Week 6 Day 5

If you haven't already, now is the time to start a bedtime routine.

Creating a bedtime routine gives your little one consistency to their day and prepares them for a long sleep. By consistently sticking to a bedtime routine, they know what's coming next and that they are winding down for bed, which gives them security and ultimately a more relaxed and happy bedtime.

Bathtime isn't just about getting clean, it's also a sensory experience for your baby and a way for them to move freely and exert some energy before going to bed.

Giving your baby a bath followed by a massage and a lovely feed each evening will help them to settle into the night.

Your baby's evening routine could look like this:

- Nappy-free time on a playmat
- Bath
- Massage
- Feed
- Cuddles and bed

FACT Research shows that bathtime is important for your baby's cognitive and emotional development. By engaging their senses, such as touch and smell, it encourages their brain to focus.

Week 6 Day 6

Sensory development is a really important part of our little ones' everyday learning and something I'd love you to promote and encourage.

Your baby will use their five senses – touch, taste, smell, sight and hearing – to fathom the world around them.

You are probably already incorporating sensory activities into your little one's daily routine without even knowing it but here is some more inspiration:

- Touch: This is the main sensory experience for newborns; they love skin-to-skin contact and being soothed by rhythmic pats. Use your finger to stroke their cheeks and around their face.
- Taste: Babies can recognise familiar tastes such as the milk they drink and can even distinguish changes in tastes such as breastmilk vs formula.
- Smell: Babies generally dislike strong perfumes.
- Sight: Your baby's eyesight will develop significantly in the first few months of life, so continue to show them high-contrast toys and images.
- Hearing: Babies love to listen to your voice and will respond to noises around them. Simply playing music in their room is a sensory experience for them.

ACTIVITY Hold your hand above your little one when they are lying down or in your arms and make shapes with your hands and fingers, pretending to be different animals such as a spider or a fish, while making a variety of sounds and expressions. Talk about how the crocodile goes 'snap, snap, snap' and the fish goes 'whooosh' through the water.

7 Weeks Old

Have a look through your little one's clothes and take out any that are now too small. Isn't it incredible how much they have grown in just forty-nine days? If you know this is your last baby and you won't be needing these clothes again, you could gift them to a friend who is expecting or find a local charity shop to donate them to.

FACT Until the age of six months old, newborns have a natural breath-holding reflex and are able to hold their breath underwater and even adapt their heart rate.

A professional, well-trained swimming instructor will be able to teach your little one to use this technique, so if you want a little water baby, now is the time to book a course.

FOOD FOR THOUGHT Avocado aids healthy digestion, promotes brain function and is also rich in vitamin C. Try avocado on toast this morning for an energy-boosting breakfast.

ACTIVITY Babies love bright lights and watching the movement and shadows that light projectors make. Try one in their room: the light can calm a fractious baby or distract a wriggling one while they have their nappy changed! Babies can watch the patterns on the ceiling from their playmat. I also find it helps babies enjoy tummy time while they watch the shapes the light creates on the floor.

Week 7 Day 1

Let's talk about overtiredness . . .

Your baby needs regular sleep throughout the day to be able to grow and thrive, and so that they are happy and alert when awake.

If your baby is crying because they're overtired, swaddle them and tuck them into their cot or pram. They might continue to cry for a few minutes but will settle quicker than if they are kept up or cuddled to stop the crying and then put down. If you do the latter you will find you spend ten minutes settling them, then when you put them down they cry again. The cycle continues, which results in your baby getting more and more tired.

Sometimes babies cry because they're tired and then the cry escalates and they don't know how to stop. They end up crying uncontrollably even though they've forgotten what they were originally crying for!

FACT Babies have a stress response to being tired. Their brain thinks there must be a reason why they need to stay awake, so releases the hormone cortisol, which has a stimulating, wake-up effect. This makes it harder for babies to sleep, leading to broken nights and tricky nap times – so follow the correct routine for your baby's age to make sure they don't get overtired.

TIP If your baby won't settle, try wrapping them in a blanket and holding them near a loud running tap. The water acts as a distracting white noise and you can even wet their hair and massage their head with a soft sponge to calm them.

Thought of the day: you don't have to be a perfect mum to be a great mum.

ACTIVITY Find a moment to tell your little one why you believe they are the most special baby in the world.

TIP Throughout your baby's childhood, smile at them to give them confidence in situations where they might be feeling worried or unsure. I always smile at babies when I lay them in their cot to send the message that all is well and that their bed is a safe and happy place.

Week 7 Day 3

FACT Babies are sick! Some babies suffer from reflux once a week, but most are sick on a daily basis and some are sick several times per feed.

Quite often babies can be very sicky, but it doesn't seem to bother or affect them at all, and they continue to put on weight and thrive. If this is the case, the reflux could be due to an under-developed digestive system and it's only a hindrance to you, not your baby, as it means a lot of laundry!

Babies' digestive systems are new to everything. If you have a baby who happily takes a feed and then sicks up a little blob while winding, that's completely normal and nothing to worry about.

Lots of people understandably worry about their baby being sick, and often presume the whole feed has been brought up. Remember that sick goes a long way and there often appears to be more than there actually is!

When to seek help:

- Your baby is not putting on weight
- They have dry nappies
- Their vomit contains blood
- They are unsettled during feeds

ACTIVITY Do the milk test at home to help you gauge how much your baby is sicking up: simply pour a little milk onto a teaspoon and throw it over your jeans – it goes *everywhere*, but it is only a teaspoon!

TIP Keep your little one upright after a feed, either by holding them or putting them in an inclined bouncy chair. This will help them digest their milk and make them less likely to be sick.

Week 7 Day 4

MINDFULNESS When making a cup of tea, hear the water bubbling and boiling in the kettle, watch the steam rise, smell the aroma, notice the movement of the water as you stir the spoon through the water and the change in colour as the tea brews. When you hold the mug, feel the warmth go through your hands and fingers. Sip slowly and enjoy every mouthful!

FACT Your baby is already able to pick up on stress. They pick up on your facial expressions and tone of voice and can be unsettled if you seem upset.

TIP Practise the art of slowing down rather than speeding up in stressful situations. When your baby gets distressed or starts to cry, your response might be to speed up. For example, when your baby starts to grumble in the pram, instead of walking faster, causing your heart rate to rise, make a conscious effort to slow yourself down. The more relaxed you are with your baby, especially in response to their crying, the more likely they are to calm. The same applies when in the car. When your baby cries, remember they are safe and can come to no harm, so continue to drive at the same speed and talk to them in a slow and calming tone.

ACTIVITY You will soon notice your baby being able to track moving objects with their eyes, an important part of their development. To encourage this, hold a toy in front of them, rattle it to catch their attention and then move it slowly from side to side and see if they follow.

Week 7 Day 5

By now, your baby has discovered there is more to life than eating and sleeping. They should be able to stay awake for longer periods now, allowing more time for play and interaction between you.

FOOD FOR THOUGHT To help keep your energy levels up, snack on dried apricots which are full of iron.

MINDFULNESS As you pass a mirror for the first time today, take a big breath and smile at your reflection. Think of something or someone who makes you smile and set your day off to a positive start!

ACTIVITY Try lying tummy to tummy. Position your little one on you so their tummy is touching your chest. Lean back so that you are both comfortable, keeping both hands on your baby at all times. Chat or sing to them and see if they can lift their head to follow the sound of your voice. You are taking the pressure off the back of their heads, and they often find the pressure on their tummy soothing if they have any trapped wind. This activity helps strengthen their head, neck and back and is an alternative way to practise traditional tummy time.

Week 7 Day 6

Flat head syndrome happens because a newborn baby's skull is quite soft and can change shape if there is a constant pressure on a specific point of the head. Because we now know that for safety, babies must sleep on their backs, more babies develop flat heads because they spend so many hours a day with pressure on the back of their head.

There are two types – plagiocephaly, where the head is flat on one side and brachycephaly where the back of the head becomes flat. In both cases, it will develop over time and won't cause your baby any pain or discomfort.

How to avoid flat head syndrome:

- Practise lots of tummy time.
- Limit the amount of time your baby is in their car seat.
- Throughout the day, alternate the side of the mattress on which your baby sleeps in their cot or pram. This prevents pressure points in the mattress where your baby lies. Use a rolled towel to tuck down the side they are sleeping on so that you remember to switch it over to the other side at the next nap time.

FACT It is estimated that 46 per cent of newborns are born with or develop a flat area on their head within the first few months of life, but it doesn't cause any harm to their development or their brain.

8 Weeks Old

Your baby is due their first set of vaccinations in the next week or so – have you got these booked in? I believe it is important to have your baby vaccinated to protect not only your baby, but others too.

Remember to take your red book with you and ask your doctor to fill it in once they have been done. Also make sure you buy infant paracetamol before the appointment and have a thermometer handy.

The doctor will ask you to hold your baby on your lap facing forwards. Talk to them in an upbeat, calm voice so they don't become anxious, while holding their arms securely so they are nice and still. The injection will be done in seconds and your baby will cry, usually after a little two-second delay. Once the doctor is finished, bring your baby up to your shoulder for a big cuddle and comfort. Tell them it's OK and all finished, using a shushing noise to calm them. I usually stand up and walk around the room to show them something out the window as a distraction. They should very quickly forget all about it.

If it's near a feed time, find a nice place to feed them – then you can both heave a sigh of relief that it's all done!

Your little one may react to some vaccinations and feel unwell with a temperature afterwards. The side effects should only last a few days, so keep them as comfortable as possible with lots of TLC during this period, giving infant paracetamol if needed (this is safe to give to babies once they are two months old). They may want to feed little and often.

FACT Vaccinations are offered to every baby in the UK free of charge.

TIP Dress your baby in comfortable clothing which is easy to remove and put back on, or allows the doctor to reach the area where the injection is going.

Week 8 Day 1

Once your baby has established a good four-hour routine, you might want to drop a feed to enable your baby (and you!) to sleep longer at night. The first feed that you will want to drop is either the 11 p.m. or the 3 a.m. feed. This is usually at around eight weeks old. You have two options:

1. Put your baby to bed at 7 p.m. and let them sleep for as long as they can without waking them. They usually wake at around 1 a.m. to begin with. Give them a big feed when they wake so they can get as close to the morning feed as possible. They will sometimes wake at 5 or 6 a.m.; if they do, offer a small feed and tuck them back into bed for another sleep before you start the day at 7 a.m. The benefit of this is that you can go to bed early and don't have to wait up to do the last feed.
2. Alternatively, feed your baby at 11 p.m. and see if they can stretch until 6.30 a.m. If they wake before 6 a.m., do the same as above; offer a small feed and tuck them back into bed for a sleep before you start the day at 7 a.m. Continuing the dream feed at 11 p.m. or letting them have their longer stretch of sleep in the evening is a personal preference. I have done it both ways. Personally, I find letting them stretch as far as they can after bedtime makes it easier for babies to get to 7 a.m. without having a second feed. But discuss it with your partner as you may strike a deal that they don't mind staying up and feeding the baby at 11 p.m. and let you go to bed . . . meaning you could be sleeping for a whole night!

FOOD FOR THOUGHT If you are breastfeeding, you might experience some discomfort if your baby is sleeping for longer spells at night. Your body will soon tune in to your little one's new routine and your milk supply will adjust accordingly. However, if you are in pain, you can take painkillers and express a little bit to relieve the swelling.

Week 8 Day 2

Around this time, your little one will become disturbed by bright lights and noise such as televisions while they are trying to sleep.

Once you have finished your bedtime routine with your baby, I would put them in their Moses basket to sleep so that they can get quality sleep without being disturbed. This also allows you to enjoy your evening without feeling you have to tiptoe around them. Make sure you set up a monitor so you can hear them, and check on your baby regularly until you join them when you go to sleep.

FACT Babies and children exposed to televisions in the two hours before bedtime are more likely to have disrupted sleep patterns due to overstimulation.

FOOD FOR THOUGHT Try my No-Bake Energy Balls recipe . . . a perfect snack if you're on the go or to eat during night feeds. You can keep them in an airtight container in the fridge for up to one week, or they can be frozen for up to three months.

Ingredients
6 tablespoons peanut butter
5 tablespoons honey
125g rolled oats
85g toasted shredded coconut
85g chocolate chips (milk, white or dark)

1. Heat the peanut butter and honey in a pan.
2. Pour into a large bowl then add all the rest of the ingredients, stirring to combine.
3. Cover the mixing bowl and chill for 1–2 hours.
4. Once the mixture is chilled, roll into 2cm balls.

Week 8 Day 3

If you start to notice some patches of yellow scabs or crust on your baby's head, forehead or eyebrows, it will probably be cradle cap. It is a very common and harmless skin condition and can develop any time during your little one's first two years. No one knows the cause – some think it is a build-up of dead skin cells, while others believe it is due to the production of too much sebum, an oily substance that forms naturally in the sebaceous glands.

Cradle cap isn't harmful to your baby and won't bother them, but it's unsightly and if it really takes hold your baby's hair can fall out with the scabs, so it's best to treat it in the early stages with a natural remedy – coconut oil and massage. The trick to beating cradle cap is to catch it early and moisturise! The condition starts by looking like a patch of dry skin, so as soon as you see any signs of dry skin on your baby's head, massage coconut oil over the area in circular motions to try to break down the scabs. You can use olive oil if you prefer, but coconut oil smells better and I have found it to be more effective.

FACT Cradle cap is not contagious and is not caused by poor hygiene.

TIP Leave the oil on overnight and if your baby has lots of hair that looks greasy, wash it off in the morning with a baby shampoo. You can use a soft-bristled hairbrush during the day to massage and stimulate the area.

REMINDER Here is a reminder to take your monthly photo today of your baby alongside your chosen teddy bear. This is number two of your twelve photographs, which you can keep to document your little one's growth during their first year.

Week 8 Day 4

If you had a straightforward vaginal birth, start doing pelvic tilt exercises to make your lower abdomen stronger. To do this:

- Lie on your back with your knees bent and your feet flat on the floor.
- Put both hands on your tummy.
- Tighten your tummy muscles and push your back towards the floor.
- Squeeze your bottom tightly.
- Count to five, then relax.
- Try to repeat ten to fifteen times.

Speak to your midwife before doing this exercise.

ACTIVITY Write down your favourite memory of the past eight weeks and add it to your memory box.

FOOD FOR THOUGHT It's around this time that many bottle-fed babies need to move on to the next teat size. If you notice your baby starting to take longer to finish a feed, sucking harder than usual or getting bored and not finishing a full feed, move up to the next teat size.

FACT The average weight of a two-month-old baby girl is 5.1kg (11.3lbs), while the average weight for a baby boy is 5.6kg (12.3lbs). The average height is 57cm (22.5 inches) for girls and 58.5cm (23 inches) for boys.

Week 8 Day 5

Singing repetitive nursery rhymes over the next year will improve your baby's cognitive development, memory and concentration. Due to the pattern of their short verses, nursery rhymes are easy for your little one to recognise and remember.

ACTIVITY Think of your favourite rhyme or song from your childhood and sing it to your little one. 'Twinkle Twinkle Little Star' is a classic nursery rhyme – remember to use your hands to imitate the twinkling star.

Twinkle, twinkle, little star,
How I wonder what you are!
Up above the world so high,
Like a diamond in the sky.
Twinkle, twinkle, little star,
How I wonder what you are!

FACT The term 'nursery rhyme' comes from the book *Rhymes for the Nursery* by Jane and Ann Taylor, published in 1806. The two sisters also wrote 'The Star'.

Week 8 Day 6

The responsibility of parenthood is a lot to take on for someone who might feel as exhausted as if they have just run a marathon (or ten), and it's very common to feel a bit low in the first few months after giving birth. You are sixty-two days into sleep deprivation now, so it's totally acceptable if you're not feeling 100 per cent yourself. For the majority of parents these are normal feelings; however, be aware it could be something more, such as postnatal depression.

FACT In the UK, it's estimated that as many as 20 per cent of women and 10 per cent of men can experience anxiety or depression during the early stages of parenthood – whether it's their first, second, third or eighth child.

Here are the common signs and symptoms of postnatal depression:

- Persistent low mood, or constant elation
- Tearfulness
- Despair
- Feeling numb
- Withdrawing from social occasions
- Feelings of inadequacy
- No longer finding pleasure in things you would normally enjoy
- Loss or increase in appetite
- Feelings of guilt, shame or hopelessness
- Feeling overly anxious about your baby
- Feeling a lack of interest in your baby
- Doubt over bonding with your baby

If you do recognise symptoms of postnatal depression in yourself or your partner, it's vital to seek professional help as soon as possible, ask loved ones for support, and avoid blaming yourself in any way. The first step is to book an appointment with your GP.

9 Weeks Old

Your baby cannot talk to you yet, but they are communicating with you in many other ways. You can see this in the way your baby gets excited and moves their arms and legs, their facial expressions, their crying and cooing.

When you get your baby dressed in the morning, chat to them about what you're going to do today. Allow breaks in your conversation for them to gurgle back to you. By asking a question and then pausing, this will encourage your baby to respond and teach them about taking turns in conversation.

TIP When your baby is making cooing noises, don't interrupt them; wait until they've stopped talking while maintaining eye contact to show them you are listening. This is the start of your baby learning the art of conversation.

FACT Studies show that the more physically and actively a baby communicates, the better they will verbally communicate.

ACTIVITY Sing the classic nursery rhyme 'Hickory Dickory Dock', accentuating the words in bold so they hear the different tones of your voice. While singing the last line, move your head from side to side, smiling and looking at your baby to see if they react to this movement.

Hickory dickory dock. The mouse went up the clock
The clock struck one. The mouse went down
Hickory dickory dock
Tick tock, tick tock, tick tock, tick tock

Week 9 Day 1

Think about the family traditions that you had in your childhood. Which ones hold the fondest memories for you and why? Are any of them something you would like to continue for your baby?

It is said that family traditions increase a child's sense of security and emotional wellbeing.

Take photos of these moments to build your little one's childhood story. These photographs will also document their growth and development over the years. This could be something as simple as always having a photograph with their cousins on the same set of steps each Christmas.

Talk to your partner about their traditions and what's important for them to continue onto the next generation, and also have a think about new ones that you would like to create for your own family. This could be a trip to the seaside with a group of friends at a certain time of year, or Sunday lunch at Easter followed by an Easter egg hunt. These small moments create wonderful childhood memories.

ACTIVITY Print out a photograph of your baby with their family and write on the back the date and who everyone is. In years to come, this will be priceless.

REMINDER This is your reminder to write a letter to your little one to add to their memory box. Include any developmental milestones, places you have visited and people you have met.

Week 9 Day 2

It's good to know the five areas of your baby's development so you can encourage their learning.

- Cognitive development is their brain development: you can encourage this by playing classical music during their awake time.
- Social and emotional development: you can encourage this by frequently smiling at your little one and giving them reassurance during new experiences.
- Speech and language development: you can encourage this by talking and singing to them face to face.
- Fine motor skills are their coordination of small muscle movements between their eyes, hands and fingers: you can encourage this by giving them a small toy to grip in their hands.
- Gross motor skills are their coordination of large muscle movements such as their arms, legs and torso: you can encourage this by laying your baby on their playmat and encouraging them to reach for their toys.

Although these are the five individual areas of your baby's development, they are all interlinked. Throughout your baby's future development, you may notice that certain skills will dominate at different times. For example, it's rare that your baby's speech development will come on dramatically while they are also learning a big skill such as walking.

Week 9 Day 3

Let's talk about immunity.

FACT Your baby's immune system isn't fully developed but will get stronger throughout their first year.

In the UK it's currently recommended to sterilise your baby's bottles for twelve months.

TIP Keep a designated bowl by your kitchen sink where your bottles or breast pump parts can soak in soapy water until you have enough for a full sterilising load. This stops old milk sitting in bottles, parts from going missing, keeps your sink clutter-free and means you are not constantly running lots of sterilising cycles.

Use a bottle brush to thoroughly clean each bottle part and then rinse before putting in the steriliser.

FOOD FOR THOUGHT Your immune system is as important as your baby's. Try my Vitamin C-Boosting Smoothie recipe. Vitamin C is not only great at warding bugs off, it also helps rebalance hormones.

Ingredients

2 oranges, peeled
Frozen pineapple, a few chunks
Frozen mango, a few chunks
Coconut water, enough to reach your desired consistency
2 tablespoons plain yoghurt
1 teaspoon honey

Blitz together and serve, adding more coconut water if you like a thinner consistency.

Week 9 Day 4

Whatever the weather, I always take little ones out for a daily walk. As I've mentioned before, I believe babies who have daily fresh air sleep better at night. Being outdoors is a sensory experience for them, providing them with a change of scenery, and I feel it's beneficial for both you and your baby's mental and physical health.

TIP Try to see the world from your baby's point of view. When out and about in the pram, if your baby is awake and you are in a nice, shady area, put the hood down so they can see what's above them. The shapes, patterns and colours . . . it's all fascinating to them. It stimulates their curiosity and interest in the world around them and keeps them happy and settled. It also encourages their cognitive development to start processing and I'm pretty sure it fires something in their imagination too.

MINDFULNESS Try this visualisation exercise. To relax and unwind before you go to sleep, take yourself away to your perfect destination. Imagine being on a beach with the warm sun on your body and the sound of the waves crashing. Take some deep breaths and relax your body as you sink into a happy, relaxed state.

Week 9 Day 5

Touch is one of your baby's most important senses. It allows them to gather information about the people and things in the world around them. Direct contact on their skin is a sensory sensation. Research shows that touch builds an emotional connection and is a fundamental part of a baby's social communication.

FACT Affection causes the release of oxytocin, otherwise known as the love hormone. This helps nurture the feeling of trust between you and your baby and reduces their cortisol levels, the stress hormone. It's said that just twenty seconds of physical affection is enough to trigger the release of oxytocin.

'The sense of touch is more important for our survival than seeing, hearing, smelling and tasting.'
Professor Martin Grunwald, experimental psychologist

ACTIVITY Every night, before your little one goes to bed, I'd love you to give your baby a 'face tickle'. After their feed, gently stroke all around their face using your fingertips. From the top of their forehead down to their chin, and round their cheeks, between their eyebrows and down over their nose. The pressure point between your baby's eyebrows is called the third eye and is specifically known for helping restlessness. At the end of your face tickle, use one of your fingers to massage this spot gently in circular motions.

This face tickle will become part of their bedtime routine and is a great sleep cue as they wind down at the end of the evening.

Week 9 Day 6

Even though your little one is not even three months old yet, it's never too early to talk about their speech and language development.

Parentese is the term we use to describe how adults alter their voice to attract their baby's attention, often using a higher pitch and sing-song tone.

When talking to your baby, think of speaking in a slow and stretchy voice to over-accentuate words. Repetition is key and is a big part of their learning, so although you may think your repetitive chat is quite boring, it's not to your baby.

FACT Repetition increases your baby's confidence and strengthens the connections in their brain, which help them learn.

TIP Here are three ways to use repetition in your daily routine:

- When greeting your little one when they wake, repeat the phrase 'Good morning, what a great sleep you just had' while they adjust to the light and have a stretch.
- Sing the nursery rhyme 'Five Little Ducks' every time your baby has a bath.
- Say 'Night night, sleep tight' before you put them down to bed.

10 Weeks Old

As a new parent, it's important that you are eating well and drinking plenty of water to stay hydrated.

Here are my top tips to help you eat more healthily and take the hassle out of meal preparation:

- Make a meal plan for the week ahead. This will not only help you see if you have a varied diet, but also save you money as food won't be going to waste.
- If you make a salad, try making enough for two days. The second half can be put in an airtight container in the fridge.
- Make a batch of your favourite soup and freeze it in smaller portions. Soups can be packed with nutrients and are easy to defrost and heat up for lunch.

ACTIVITY Visit your local supermarket with your little one. They can stay in their car seat in the trolley and will enjoy looking at the lights and hustle and bustle around them. Make sure you bring an extra layer of clothing or a blanket with you as supermarkets are always cold!

FOOD FOR THOUGHT Remember, if you are breastfeeding, you might experience some discomfort in your breasts if your baby is sleeping for longer spells at night. If you are in pain, you can take painkillers and express a little bit to relieve the swelling.

Week 10 Day 1

A big part of your little one's social and emotional development is creating bonds with family and friends. Your child is too young to experience separation anxiety at the moment so I think it's good to give them the confidence of being held by others and not just you, so that when they are older, it's not a new and scary experience for them.

This also allows you to have a little break if you have willing babysitters!

ACTIVITY Your baby is getting stronger and may be able to push themselves up with their forearms during tummy time. This enables them to look around, so place some brightly coloured toys at eye level to encourage them to practise their gross motor skills by stretching and reaching out.

FOOD FOR THOUGHT Try making some fruit-infused water today. It tastes delicious, is really refreshing and will encourage you to drink more water throughout the day. Fruits to use include: lemons, limes, strawberries, chopped apples, cucumber, satsumas, raspberries, pineapple, watermelon and peaches. Mint leaves and ginger also work well.

To make it, simply fill a jug or glass bottle with water then add your sliced fruit. Keep chilled in the fridge.

Week 10 Day 2

Although your little one won't have any memory of these early days, the experiences they have from birth will shape their personalities and make them into the person they become.

Breaking the pattern of everyday life is really good for the soul and a happy parent will make a happy baby. Sometimes a change of scenery is good for everyone. When in a new location, you feel more energised and excited. This goes for you and your baby.

Watching your baby experience their 'firsts' in life is uplifting and another way to bond with your baby.

I'd like you to create a list of things that you would like to experience with your baby before their first birthday. Here are some ideas of things you could add to your list:

- Stroke an animal
- Feel the grass on your toes
- See the sea
- Have a picnic
- Visit a museum
- Ride on a train
- Swim
- Blow bubbles
- Build a sandcastle
- Feed the ducks
- Sit in a swing
- Touch snow
- Show them the moon

Week 10 Day 3

Now your baby's core and head strength is getting stronger, you can start to hold them in different positions. When you are walking around, place your baby over your shoulder, making sure one hand is always behind their head and neck, and show them the different shapes and patterns on your walls. This could be a collage of photographs, shadows on a wall or patterned curtains. This will encourage your baby to elevate their head and turn to see the different shapes and patterns.

Hold your baby outwards, with their back against your tummy, so they can observe the world around them. Take them to the window and talk to them about what's outside. This is a great distraction if you have an unhappy baby.

FACT The spine is made up of thirty-three bones. As your baby grows, their spine starts to curve into a C-shape and will eventually develop into a S-shape once they begin to crawl and walk.

ACTIVITY Make a print of your baby's hands in some air-drying clay and create some keepsakes to help you remember just how tiny those fingers were. This is a sensory play for your baby and makes great gifts for grandparents, godparents and friends.

HOW TO Roll out the clay to the desired thickness and take your baby's hand to the clay to make the print, applying pressure very gently. Have some wipes ready to clean their hands after! Trim off the edges round the handprint using a ruler so you make a neat square. Leave for a couple of days for the clay to harden completely then you can paint it or put it in a frame.

Week 10 Day 4

Your baby will now start to recognise familiar music if it's played often, so remember to sing nursery rhymes throughout the day and keep adding to your playlist.

Your baby will be happier and more content on their playmat if they can hear music playing in the background, as it gives them a sense of not being alone.

ACTIVITY Studies have proven that babies are born with an innate sense of rhythm and an instinctive ability to respond to the tempo of the music they hear. Put your baby in a carrier and have a little dance together – you could even do this with your partner. As they grow and can face outwards, they will begin to enjoy this more and more.

FACT Your baby's ears play an important role in their understanding and exploration of the world around them. Through their ears, they are able to hear vibrations as sound, which helps them learn to talk and plays a big part in their balance as they learn to crawl and walk later on.

TIP Don't forget to clean and moisturise behind your baby's ears regularly. It's a place that often gets forgotten, and an area where dirt builds up and the skin can get quite dry and flaky. Use a cotton bud soaked in coconut oil to clean the area behind their ear lobe and moisturise each evening after bathtime.

Week 10 Day 5

Your baby's nap times should stay roughly the same every day. My advice is to plan one of their naps to be undisturbed in their cot, in a nice dark room, but the other two naps can be out and about in the car or pram. It's a well-known fact that babies who nap better during the day sleep better at night. This is because an overtired baby finds it harder to settle and fall into a deep sleep.

By sticking to a routine during the day, you should avoid the dreaded 'witching hour' that people talk about before bedtime. By following a routine with the right awake-time windows, your baby won't be overtired and will be able to settle better at bedtime.

FOOD FOR THOUGHT If you are breastfeeding and you notice your baby is fussy or particularly windy after some feeds, keep a food diary to see if there is a correlation between certain foods that you eat and their unhappiness. Common foods that have been known to cause tummy upset are curry, citrus fruits, onion, fizzy drinks, caffeine and garlic.

MINDFULNESS Do you find being stuck at a red light frustrating? Next time you have to stop, instead of just willing the light to turn green, loosen your shoulders, notice your breathing and look around you to see and hear what other people are doing. Try to enjoy those few seconds and take a breather, rather than having impatient thoughts.

Week 10 Day 6

Having a baby is time-consuming!

If you are finding that you need more hours in the day, here are three tips to help:

- Cook some of your favourite meals en masse and freeze extra portions so you have meals that are easy to just put in the oven in the evenings.
- Order your groceries online to save time going to a supermarket.
- Get into the habit of putting a wash on every morning so it doesn't build up.

Consider each tiny task that you complete a big win. Try not to do too much each day or feel guilty if you don't achieve everything on your to-do list. Take time out when your little one is sleeping to enjoy a hot drink and a moment of calm.

FACT Research shows that if you have a twenty-minute nap in the afternoon, it is more restful than a twenty-minute nap in the morning.

FOOD FOR THOUGHT Have a snack of blueberries this afternoon. They are full of antioxidants and will help boost your energy levels.

11 Weeks Old

You might be experiencing postpartum back pain. This is caused by your uterus expanding during pregnancy, weakening your abdominal muscles and therefore putting extra pressure on your back.

Gentle exercise will strengthen your core and aid your recovery. Try incorporating this simple child's pose stretch into your day. With your hands and knees on the ground, sink back through your hips to your heels. Extend your arms in front of your body with your palms facing downwards, so you feel the stretch along the length of your spine. Focus on breathing, relaxing any areas of tension or tightness. Hold this pose for up to one minute.

It's important to keep your back strong and healthy, especially now that you are doing a lot of lifting and your little one is only going to get bigger.

The correct way to lift your little one is by bending your knees rather than bending from your waist. When standing back up, bring your baby close to your chest and use your legs rather than your back, as it's your leg muscles rather than your back muscles that should be doing the work.

When you are putting your baby in their car seat, kneel in front of them to strap them in, rather than bending down.

FACT A rucksack over both your shoulders is better for your back than carrying a baby bag over one shoulder. This is due to the weight being spread evenly across your body, with the strongest muscles – the back and abdominal muscles – supporting the bag.

Week 11 Day 1

Your little one's hands will probably be their favourite toy at the moment and you might find they are opening and closing them repeatedly, as well as reaching out to feel different textures and objects within reach.

Observe your baby and see if they naturally keep their fists clenched a lot of the time. If they do, encourage them to open up their hands and use your fingers to touch and stroke their palms, which will desensitise the area and stop them from being nervous when they start exploring different textures in the future.

ACTIVITY Use different objects from around the house to stroke all over the insides of your baby's hands. This is a heightened sensory experience for your baby, so build up the amount of time that you spend doing it, depending on their response and if they like the sensation or find it over-stimulating. You can use objects such as a makeup brush, a sponge, a piece of ribbon or a feather.

FACT Your breasts will change size during the first few months post-birth regardless of whether you are breastfeeding or bottle feeding.

I would recommend that you go and get yourself re-measured to be sure that you are wearing the correct bra size. If your bra is too tight, it may affect your milk supply and put pressure in the wrong areas, which can cause blocked milk ducts.

Even if you aren't breastfeeding, I recommend you are re-measured, as breast shape and size changes after pregnancy so it's likely you will need some new bras.

Week 11 Day 2

FACT Spinach contains phytoestrogens, making it an excellent food to increase your breastmilk production. It is also rich in iron, calcium, folate and vitamin K. As well as benefiting your milk production it will also improve your skin, hair and bone health.

FOOD FOR THOUGHT Try my delicious Spinach Soup recipe for a healthy lunch. This recipe makes four portions.

Ingredients
25g butter
1 bunch spring onion, chopped
1 leek, sliced
1 small potato, peeled and cut in half
2 sticks of celery, chopped
1 litre vegetable stock
450g spinach
50g peas, fresh or frozen
freshly ground black pepper

1. Heat the butter in a large pan and add the spring onion, leek, potato and celery to sweat for ten minutes.
2. Add the stock and cook for 10–15 minutes until the potato is cooked through.
3. Add the spinach and peas and cook for a few minutes until the spinach has wilted and the peas are cooked through.
4. Grind over plenty of black pepper, blitz with a blender and serve!

TIP Try adding spinach to your omelettes, salads and smoothies.

Week 11 Day 3

FACT Your baby is starting to see in colour now and is also seeing the world around them in 3D.

Your face is still their favourite thing to look at and they will be fascinated by your changing facial expressions. Spend ten minutes today making silly faces and different sounds to see which ones your baby reacts to most positively.

ACTIVITY Babies love the feel and colour of ribbons. Hang short ribbons (under 20cm) from your baby's playmat or tie them to a teething toy for them to admire the colours and feel the silky material – though keep safety concerns in mind and never leave your baby unsupervised.

MINDFULNESS It's important to remember your own parenting milestones as well as your baby's. What used to be simple tasks, such as getting out of the house, meeting friends for a coffee or doing the weekly shop are now no mean feat! I think all parents recognise this, so conquering these tasks should be celebrated and you should be proud of yourself.

Week 11 Day 4

ACTIVITY For a bit of fun, spend some time today researching your baby's astrology. Write down:

- Their star sign and what it says about their personality
- Their birthstone
- The meaning behind their name
- Which flower and tree represents your baby's birth month
- Which animal they are according to the Chinese lunar calendar year

Add this to your little one's memory box.

FACT As your baby gets bigger, their bowel gets bigger too, which means they will start to have fewer bowel movements.

Week 11 Day 5

I believe you can never have too many photographs of your baby. They change so quickly in the first few months, so I recommend you take plenty to treasure.

TIP Here are my top tips for capturing some special shots:

- Warm it up. Make sure the room you are in is warm and your baby isn't cold, especially if you plan on stripping your baby down for photographs. I sometimes use a plug-in radiator to boost the temperature if needed, particularly during the winter months!
- Choose a good time. You know your baby better than anybody, so choose a time in the day when they will be at their best. Early morning is often a favourite when they are wide awake and alert.
- Finding the best light. Getting the light falling on your baby from the right direction is perhaps the most important factor in getting a professional-looking shot of your little one. Use the light coming in from a window or door; you want it to fall on your baby from the top of the head downwards towards their feet, so lay your baby down on a bed, sofa or the floor with the top of their head pointing towards the source of the light. You should be able to see a little shadow under your baby's nose! This also applies when photographing your baby being held by a parent or sibling.
- Never shoot from below. Position your camera level with your baby's nose or above to get the most flattering shot. You want to take your photograph from above your baby looking down towards their feet, and not from below so you can see up their nostrils.

Week 11 Day 6

This might surprise you, but I don't actually believe colic exists. It's a term used to describe an unhappy baby who cries for periods throughout the day, but it doesn't actually describe a medical condition. Instead of just labelling your baby as having colic, look for signs of what is causing them the discomfort so you can take the right steps to make them feel better.

If a baby is unsettled it might be because they are:

- Overtired
- Hungry
- Have trapped wind
- Have a tongue-tie (see page 14) so find it hard to latch, which in turn creates wind
- Have reflux (see page 77)
- Have a digestive issue such a cow's milk protein allergy (see page 240, though please note: babies can be given cow's milk mixed in food from around six months, but wait until they are a year old before giving it as a drink)

If your baby is crying a lot and there seems to be no obvious cause, please see a doctor or other medical professional to rule out any medical conditions.

TIP Try the carrying position (see illustration on page 16) known as the 'tiger in the tree' hold. If your baby has trapped wind or tummy ache, it's a good one to try as they find it very comfortable and relaxing. Just don't do it straight after a feed as they may be sick! Use either arm and bring it across your baby's front, with your hand tucked around their nappy. Use your other hand to stroke and pat their back gently and rhythmically.

12 Weeks Old

It's almost time for your baby's next set of vaccinations. On the day, remember to dress them in loose and comfortable clothing, so you can get easy access to their legs.

After their vaccinations, you may find they are restless at night, or more clingy during the day. The side effects should only last a few days, so keep them as comfortable as possible with lots of TLC. They may also want to feed more often during the day.

If your baby reacted to their first set of vaccinations, it doesn't necessarily mean they will have the same reaction the second time, so go in with an open mind.

TIP Once a month, air your baby's mattress by taking the sheet off and standing it up in the cot for an hour. When putting the mattress back in the cot, turn it round the opposite way to how it was before, to avoid pressure points in the mattress where your baby lies.

Week 12 Day 1

If your body feels good you can now introduce some impact exercises like running or gentle squat jumps.

ACTIVITY Try doing squats while you are on a walk with your baby in their pram. Stand in front of your pram and rest your hands on the handlebar, with your feet shoulder-width apart. Squat down to the same height as your knees, keeping your chest up and the weight in your heels. Breathe in at the top and breathe out as you go down and come back up. Aim to gradually increase how many squats you do each day.

TIP If you feel any heaviness or leaking in your pelvic floor, avoid whatever exercise is causing this. I advise going to see a pelvic health physio, as they can help with abdominal separation and the pelvic floor. If anything doesn't feel quite right – like backache, or you notice your abs bulging out when you sit up, or you're suffering from incontinence – then booking in to see a good pelvic health physio will make the world of difference.

Although urine leaking is common post-birth, it is not normal and you should not have to live with it. It can be fixed.

Week 12 Day 2

Your little one might be growing out of their newborn clothes and you might be meeting this with mixed emotions . . . isn't it incredible how much they have grown in just 86 days? The newborn phase really does fly by.

I use the expression 'pinch an inch' to determine when a little one is growing out of their babygrows. You should be able to feel about 2 cm space at the bottom of their feet to enable them to have a really good stretch. If a babygrow is too tight, it will restrict their movement and make them uncomfortable.

Once your baby outgrows their clothes, group them together in sizes and label them in bags or boxes. This keeps everything organised and easy for you to pull out, whether you want to use them again in the future or gift them.

ACTIVITY If you have any outfits that are special to you, put them in their memory box.

TIP Cut the labels out of clothes that come into direct contact with your baby's skin, such as vests and hats. As adults, we can itch and move any labels that irritate us, but babies can't do this.

Week 12 Day 3

Although your baby will still be sleeping in your room, if they have their own bedroom or nursery it's nice to make their room an inviting and stimulating place for them to spend time in. Use a lamp to create warm lighting and hang a mobile near their changing area for them to look up at. A comfortable chair in their room will create a cosy place for reading stories and feeding. Spend time in their room every day so they get used to being in the space before they make the big transition later on.

Putting a framed photograph of family members in their room will help them recognise people who are going to play a big part in their life. You can show them the photograph and point to their faces, telling them who is who. One day, your little one will be able to point each member out to you.

As a way of creating conversation with your baby while they're still so young, you could tell them funny stories about each person in the photograph. It's amazing how much language your little one will pick up from the things you chat to them about now.

FACT You might notice your baby making noises and twitching in their sleep, but this doesn't mean they are dreaming, they are simply having reflexes. They won't start having dreams until they are around two years old.

Week 12 Day 4

Meningitis is the illness we all fear and it's important you know the signs to look out for.

It can affect anyone but it is most common in babies and children. Vaccinations help protect your child from certain strains of meningitis.

Meningitis symptoms can appear in any order, with some not appearing at all. Symptoms of meningitis include:

- Fever
- Headache
- Vomiting
- Stiff neck
- Struggling to look at bright lights
- Rash that does not fade when you roll a glass over the skin
- Drowsiness
- Seizures

If you are concerned your little one has meningitis, do not hesitate to call 999.

FACT There is not always a rash, which is what most people associate with the virus, and it can be harder to see on dark skin.

REMINDER Here is a reminder to take your monthly photo today of your baby alongside your chosen teddy bear. This is number three of your twelve photographs, which you can keep to document your little one's growth during their first year.

Week 12 Day 5

Now that your baby is approaching three months old, I have put together eight milestones which you can tick off if your little one has accomplished them.

If they haven't reached all of them yet, I'm sure it's nothing to worry about, but it's a good idea to have a chat with your health visitor. Remember, every baby goes at their own pace.

1. Makes eye contact
2. Turns head to follow your voice
3. Puts hands to mouth
4. Focuses on a black and white pattern
5. Practises tummy time
6. Makes a cooing sound
7. Follows a toy when held in front of them
8. Smiles

Week 12 Day 6

Have a read through Routine 3 to see if your baby is ready to move on to it now – see pages 116 to 117.

Over the next month, hopefully your baby will be sleeping from 7 p.m. to 7 a.m. with one dream feed. Some babies will drop the dream feed between four and five months and sleep from 7 p.m. to 7 a.m. Hungrier babies will need to wait until they're weaned on to puréed food before they're happy to drop this feed.

TIP If your baby starts to refuse the dream feed or takes a very small amount, such as 60ml (2fl oz), I would stop waking them.

ACTIVITY If you have a foil blanket in your medical box, it makes a brilliant sensory mat for your baby!

Lay the blanket on a comfortable surface and let your baby enjoy the sound of the rustle and the shiny texture. They can also enjoy tummy time on the foil blanket. Some babies might not like the sound of the blanket at first, so make sure they can see you and that you smile and talk to them for reassurance while they get used to the new sounds and feeling.

Routine 3

3 to 5 Months

By three to four months old, hopefully your baby will be sleeping from 7 p.m. to 7 a.m. with one feed. Some babies will drop the feed between four and five months and sleep from 7 p.m. to 7 a.m.; hungrier babies will need to wait until they're weaned on to puréed food before they're happy to drop this feed.

7 a.m. Wake, feed, wind. Change nappy, have some nappy-off time, top and tail, moisturise and dress baby for the day. Offer a top-up.

8.45 a.m. Put down for a nap. This is a lovely time for a sleep in the pram outside.

10.30 a.m. Wake baby, enjoy some playtime together or on a playmat.

11 a.m. Feed, wind, change nappy. Offer a top-up.

12.45 a.m. Put down for a nap in their cot when at home.

3 p.m. Wake baby, feed, wind, nappy change, offer a top-up.

4 p.m. A short nap of around thirty to forty-five minutes.

5 p.m. Wake baby for some playtime.

5.45 p.m. Start bathtime with some nappy-off and tummy time. Finish bathtime with a baby massage.

6.30 p.m. Big feed and lots of time winding.

7 p.m. Bedtime. If baby has had substantial feeds during the day, they will need one feed between bedtime and the next morning (i.e. between 7 p.m. and 7 a.m.). You can carry on with the dream feed or letting baby sleep and wake on their own accord as before. The aim is to gradually reduce the amount of milk baby takes at the dream feed, or for baby to sleep longer and longer through the night, as their milk feeds get bigger in the day, until this feed is dropped altogether.

13 Weeks Old

If you notice your little one is sleeping for longer periods and is hungrier than usual, it is very possible they are going through a growth spurt. For tips on how to deal with this, see page 33.

FOOD FOR THOUGHT Just one sweet potato meets the daily recommendation of vitamin A for a breastfeeding mother. Vitamin A is important for vision, bone growth and your immune system. They make great chips – or why not try adding some to a cottage pie topping instead of the usual potato?

REMINDER This is your reminder to write a letter to your little one to add to their memory box. Include any developmental milestones, places you have visited and people you have met.

Week 13 Day 1

MINDFULNESS In moments of frustration when you need a reminder that you can cope in a stressful situation and have the power to respond in a way that you won't later regret, touch your thumb with your first finger and say the word 'CALM'. Then touch your thumb with your second finger, saying the word 'BEGINS'. With your third finger say 'WITH', and your fourth finger say 'ME'.

FOOD FOR THOUGHT Chickpeas are high in fibre, which helps sustain regular bowel movements. Research also suggests they can help lower your cholesterol.

Try my Homemade Hummus recipe:

Ingredients
200g chickpeas
2 tablespoons lemon juice
2 tablespoons olive oil
2 tablespoons tahini
1 garlic clove, crushed

1. Blend all the ingredients together, adding water until you reach a smooth consistency.
2. Serve as a dip for delicious crudités like sticks of cucumber, peppers, sugar snap peas, carrot batons and celery.

Week 13 Day 2

If you have been practising tummy time daily, your little one may now be able to lift their head a full ninety degrees when placed on their front. Continue to encourage this by placing a mirror on the floor in front of them or some brightly coloured toys and books. Having something to look at will hold their attention for longer and stop them getting bored and restless.

FACT In the first few years of life, more than 1 million new connections are formed every second in your baby's growing brain.

ACTIVITY Create two different music playlists, one for playtime and one for quieter periods, such as when your little one is sleeping in the car or winding down during the evenings. Choose child-friendly songs that you also enjoy listening to; it might be a Disney soundtrack from your own childhood or songs from your favourite musicals. The more you are able to sing along, the more fun and entertaining it is for your baby!

Week 13 Day 3

Today is all about sleeping bags.

As soon as your baby can roll over, you must take them out of their swaddle as they may roll onto their front and then be restricted.

I find babies are ready to transition from a swaddle into a sleeping bag when they are between three and four months old, ideally when they are consistently sleeping from roughly 10 p.m. to 7 a.m.

Here are my tips for making your transition a smooth one:

- Start the transition by swaddling your baby with one arm in and one arm out.
- Alternate the arm that is out of the swaddle each night.
- Fold over the inbuilt mitt on their babygrow to stop their hand getting cold.
- You might find that your baby stirs a few times in the night but hopefully they can resettle themselves.
- After a few days, transition your baby into a sleeping bag.

If you find your baby kicks and rolls around in their sleeping bag, tuck the bottom of the sleeping bag into the mattress. This will help them feel more secure.

Depending on the room temperature and how thick the sleeping bag is, your baby might need a blanket tucked in over the top of their sleeping bag to stay warm enough.

TOP TIP Remember to keep their hands covered with the inbuilt mitts to stop them scratching themselves and stop their hands getting cold.

Week 13 Day 4

It's not a nice thing to discuss, but a very important topic – have you made or altered your will since having your baby?

A will can be used to appoint a legal guardian to look after your child or children (under the age of eighteen years) in the event of your death.

To avoid your loved ones having to deal with any uncertainty as to what will happen to your children, and for your peace of mind, please make a will to ensure that your wishes will be fulfilled.

FACT Lots of parents think that if your child has a godparent, they don't need to have a named guardian – but this is not the case. Asking a friend or relative to be a godparent to your child is a huge honour, but it doesn't give them any legal rights or responsibility.

Week 13 Day 5

Do you have a nickname for your little one?

A nickname is a term of endearment that signifies love and affection, and is used to portray belonging. It could be the shortening of your baby's name or something that reminds you of them.

Some of the ones I've used are: my baby; treasure, poppet; bunny and my love.

FACT Babies can get little blisters on their lips. It is most common in the first few months and normally nothing to be concerned about. It can happen to both breastfed and bottle-fed babies. The blisters are caused by friction from sucking on the breast or bottle teat. Your baby's lips can also appear chapped and look as if they are peeling; this is also normal. Keep them well moisturised with a little coconut oil.

FOOD FOR THOUGHT If you find yourself getting a bit peckish later in the morning, try eating a few nuts or a couple of rice cakes with nut butter on top. Nut butter contains healthy fats and proteins that will help boost your energy levels and keep you satisfied until lunchtime. It is packed with minerals and vitamins such as potassium, zinc, magnesium and vitamin E.

Week 13 Day 6

I really want to stress to you today that routines are not there to be regimented or to tie you to the house.

I genuinely believe that babies thrive from having a regular feeding and sleep pattern. The babies on my routine are happy and can thrive physically and mentally because they are well fed and rested.

Routines take a bit of time and practice in the early days and I strongly advise you stick to the timings on a daily basis until your little one is feeding and sleeping well. Once they are consistently on the routine suited to their age, you can of course be more flexible.

I am a huge advocate of babies being outside and enjoying being part of the family, so on special occasions, let them be involved. Routine timings can be altered, knowing that the next day you can go straight back to it – that's the beauty of a routine.

FACT A dark environment helps your baby produce melatonin, which is known as the sleep hormone. Therefore, blackout blinds will make it easier for your little one to fall asleep.

TIP If you are out and about, try to stick to your baby's nap times so they don't get overtired. Let them sleep on the go by using a portable white noise machine and a blackout cover for the pram to recreate your baby's sleeping environment.

14 Weeks Old

FACT Your baby's hair loss will peak at around this age. It is completely normal for your baby to lose their hair. When a new growth cycle starts, the existing hair falls out.

FOOD FOR THOUGHT If you are experiencing post-partum hair loss yourself, these are foods that will help boost your hair growth: avocado, eggs, nuts, green vegetables, sweet potatoes, salmon and beans. I recommend taking a supplement; just make sure they are safe if you are breastfeeding.

TIP When brushing your baby's hair, sing a little rhyme at the same time, for example 'brush, brush, brush your hair'. This will distract them from what can be a strange feeling as they will be concentrating on your voice. Use a baby brush with soft bristles and do gentle strokes down from the root of the hair. This promotes healthy hair growth.

ACTIVITY Indulge in a hair mask this evening. If you don't have time to go to the shops, try this tried-and-tested homemade mask – it will make your hair extremely soft and silky.

You only need these two store cupboard staples: one egg and two heaped tablespoons of mayonnaise.

1. Whisk the egg and mayonnaise together to create a creamy consistency.
2. Coat all your hair with the mixture, then cover your hair with cling film or a shower cap for half an hour.
3. Brush your hair through until it is smooth and knot-free.
4. Rinse, shampoo and condition as normal.

Week 14 Day 1

If you're finding it frustrating that you can't find a free hour to do some exercise, do not worry. Even fifteen minutes of basic exercises while your baby plays on the mat beside you can make you feel energised. Consistency is key, not how long you've worked out for.

HOW TO Set your timer to fifteen minutes and do as many rounds of the following exercises as possible:

- 10 squats
- 10 tricep dips
- 10 reverse lunges
- 10 press ups on knees
- 10 slow, controlled ab rolldowns (start from a sitting position and lean back slightly as you take a deep breath out and pull your abs in – no need to go all the way down).

If these exercises feel too hard, just adjust them to your level. Maybe do five reps instead of ten or give yourself a thirty-second rest before moving on to the next exercise. Or even just do ten minutes.

Anything is better than nothing and you should always feel proud of achieving any exercise.

ACTIVITY When bathing your little one this evening, use a cup to pour water from a height all around their body to create different sensations and make bathtime into a sensory experience for them.

Week 14 Day 2

Wow, 100 days with your baby!

ACTIVITY Find a picture of your little one as a newborn in their Moses basket or pram. Take a photo today in the same spot to compare the two and marvel at just how much they have grown and changed.

FOOD FOR THOUGHT Seeds and nuts are mood-boosting foods that will help calm your nervous system and are packed with essential fatty acids, vitamins and protein.

Try my Homemade Pesto recipe:

Ingredients
70g fresh basil leaves
2 garlic cloves, peeled
50g pine nuts
100g grated Parmesan cheese
80ml olive oil

1. Put the basil and garlic in a food processor, and blend for a minute.
2. Add the pine nuts and Parmesan and keep blending while adding in the oil. Do not overwork; stop when it's at the right consistency for you.
3. If the mixture is a bit thick, add a little more oil.

This is delicious served as a pasta sauce, or with vegetables, or baked on top of salmon.

Week 14 Day 3

Teething can start at any age between three and seven months old.

Some babies don't experience any pain or side effects – suddenly, a tooth just pops through. Others can feel very poorly and suffer from teething pain for weeks.

Most babies don't start teething for another month or so, but to be prepared I would purchase some teething toys, teething gel and paracetamol.

Your little one will go through periods of teething, until they get their final molars at about three years old.

Here are some more things you may not know about your baby's teeth:

- Your child will end up with twenty teeth in total!
- Teeth usually appear in pairs.
- Milk teeth are already formed in your baby's gums when they are born, and some babies are actually born with teeth.
- Teething age is thought to be hereditary, so if you were early to get your teeth, the chances are your little one will be too!
- Teeth do not cut through the flesh. Hormones are released within the body that cause the gums to separate slightly, allowing the teeth to come through.
- Usually the bottom two middle incisors are the first to break through the gums, followed by the top two incisors.

TIP Keep teething toys in a freezer bag in the fridge. The coolness will provide extra relief on your baby's gums.

Week 14 Day 4

Creating a safe and secure sleeping space for your little one will help them self-settle and sleep more soundly. Here are some essential things to remember when putting your baby to bed:

- Your baby should always be put to sleep on their back.
- Always lay your baby at the bottom of their cot, so that their feet almost touch the end – think 'feet to foot'. This means that if you tuck them in with a blanket, they can only wriggle up and out from underneath the blanket, rather than down underneath it.
- If you do use a blanket, make sure it is tucked in tightly under each side of the mattress to stop it becoming loose.

TIP Your baby will almost definitely create stains of different delightful colours on their clothing, especially as you head closer to the weaning stage! If you have stubborn stains that are still visible after washing, sunlight is the best stain remover. Put the clothes outside in direct sunlight and prepare to be amazed as it works its magic.

FOOD FOR THOUGHT Drinking fennel tea will boost your prolactin levels, which can increase your milk supply.

Week 14 Day 5

Snacks can be a great way of consuming more nutrients – choose tasty bites made from fruits and vegetables for the healthiest options.

FOOD FOR THOUGHT Kale and spinach are superfoods packed with vitamins and folate, which promote new brain cell growth.

Try my Kale Chips recipe for a nutritious alternative to potato crisps:

Ingredients
250g kale
Olive oil
Seasoning of your choice, e.g. cayenne pepper; cinnamon; garlic powder; nutritional yeast; freshly ground black pepper
Pinch of sea salt

1. Preheat the oven to 180°C.
2. Remove the kale stems and tear the kale into smaller pieces.
3. Put the kale on a lined baking tray and spread it out as much as possible as this will make it crispier.
4. Lightly drizzle olive oil over the kale.
5. Sprinkle your choice of seasoning evenly over the kale, adding a touch of salt.
6. Put the tray in the oven for 12–15 minutes.
7. Shake the tray to separate the kale and cook for a few further minutes.
8. Remove from the oven and let the chips cool in the tray.

TIP If the kale isn't crispy enough, turn the oven off and let it sit in the oven while it cools. This will remove any excess moisture and make the chips crispier.

Week 14 Day 6

Rolling is one the first big physical milestones your baby will learn.

The more time your little one spends enjoying themselves on a playmat, with age-appropriate toys to reach and grab, the more likely they are to start rocking and then eventually rolling to the side.

Regular tummy time will also help to build up their neck, back and arm strength, all of which is needed for rolling.

It's common for babies to start by rolling from their front to their back, but it may take a few weeks longer for your baby to be able to roll from their back to their front.

When your baby first starts rolling over it may be a surprise to you both! It's not uncommon for early rolls to be exciting for parents, but a shock for babies. Comfort your little one if they cry in surprise after mastering their new skill, but reassure them by smiling and telling them how clever they are.

Once your baby can wriggle and roll, it's even more important to keep one hand on them while you change them. They should also stop being swaddled and move into a sleeping bag if they haven't transitioned already (see page 121).

You might have a few weeks of disturbed sleep where your baby rolls onto their front but is unable to roll back again, and so wakes and cries for you to pop them back.

Once your baby is able to turn themselves back over, it is perfectly safe for them to sleep on their fronts if that's what they find the most comfortable. So don't worry about turning them over and disturbing their sleep.

TIP Try tucking their sleeping bag into the bottom of the cot mattress to stop them being able to roll initially.

Some babies hardly dribble at all, some dribble when they are poorly or teething, and some babies dribble excessively and have to wear bibs at all times of the day to stop their clothes being sodden. Which is your little one?

Here are some more facts about drooling:

- Babies produce up to eight times as much saliva per day as an adult.
- Saliva contains water, salts and mucus.
- The function of saliva is to protect the mouth and throat when eating by removing bacteria and helping the digestive process.
- We have six salivary glands located in the bottom of our mouths, cheeks and near our front teeth.

Dribbling is usually caused by teething and stops once that tooth has cut through, but if you find your little one is constantly drooling, they will need to wear bibs throughout the day and have them changed regularly to stop their skin becoming irritated.

You may find your baby starts to blow bubbles soon!

TIP Bibs with plastic backs are good for stopping the wetness going through to your little one's clothing, but they're not as comfortable to wear, so I tend to have a collection of cotton 'bandana'-style bibs which become part of your baby's outfit.

Week 15 Day 1

Nappy-free time is more important for your baby than you might think.

Imagine only ever knowing the feeling of having a nappy on . . . Many toddlers find it hard to poo in the loo if they've never known the sensation of having nothing around their bottom. So, now is the time to get your little one used to having no nappy on. Here are four more reasons to try it:

- Nappy-free time will encourage your baby to kick and move more freely, using up more energy and often helping to relieve trapped wind.
- Letting your little one's skin breathe will reduce the chance of a yeast infection.
- Taking your baby's nappy off prevents nappy rash by keeping the area ventilated, clean and dry.
- If your baby is agitated or unhappy, taking their nappy off and allowing them some freedom of movement will often calm them.

ACTIVITY Try to incorporate nappy-free time throughout the day. When your baby is on their playmat, take their nappy off. When changing their nappy, instead of putting their nappy straight back on, let them have a kick and a stretch. Tummy time can also be done without a nappy on. Or why not take a towel or changing mat into the bathroom and let your little one kick nappy-free while they listen to the bathwater run?

TIP Put a towel or disposable mat under their bottom when they are nappy-free as they are more than likely to pee!

Week 15 Day 2

ACTIVITY Copy your baby's actions so that they know you're paying attention to them. If they open their mouth, coo, poke their tongue out . . . do it back to them. This encourages them to repeat the action, and repetition is known to build connections in your little one's fast-developing brain.

FACT Screens are known to decrease your melatonin levels, which control our circadian rhythm, so if you are struggling to get to sleep at night, or are finding it difficult to wake up the next morning, don't use your phone or watch TV for at least half an hour before bedtime.

FOOD FOR THOUGHT Eating two kiwi fruits one or two hours before you go to bed in the evening may improve your sleep quality and help you sleep for longer. Kiwis contain a high level of serotonin, also known as the happy hormone.

MINDFULNESS We all have tasks that become mundane and things we'd rather not do – it might be the washing, ironing, doing the washing up, etc. When you do these tasks, really focus on every tiny detail – the feeling, the smells, the sound of the Hoover, the motion of your hands while they do the activity. Think of new ways of doing the task instead of doing them on autopilot.

Week 15 Day 3

I want to talk to you about how you react to situations as a parent, and how your response will affect your little one. This applies to your baby now, and as they grow into a toddler and child.

Babies do all sorts of funny things because they haven't got control of their body – for example, they might projectile vomit after having a bottle, or they might poo in the bath! It will probably be your automatic reaction to jump up, raise your voice, panic or get flustered; however, your baby will pick up on this and become worried or frightened. So with this in mind, try your very hardest not to react when things happen. Instead, keep your hand steady on them so they feel your security; keep your voice calm and level and tell them it's all OK. By panicking, you won't reverse what's just happened but you will probably end up with a crying baby on top of the situation, so my advice is to keep calm and reassure your baby before dealing with whatever has occurred!

MINDFULNESS Say this mantra out loud, preferably while looking in the mirror: 'I don't have to be a perfect mum to be a good mum.'

Are you finding that this time is just flying by? When you are in the baby phase, it can be difficult to keep in touch with family and friends day to day and, before you know it, the weeks have flown by. Go for a nice walk with your baby for one of their naps today and use the time to catch up on the phone with a friend you haven't spoken to in a while. Staying in touch with family and friends will help you feel connected and give you the chance to talk about things that are non-baby-related.

Becoming a parent is, hopefully, totally joyous but it can also be difficult and sometimes lonely. Don't be afraid to reach out if you need someone to talk to.

FACT Studies show that having just one conversation a day with a friend has a significant positive effect on your mental health.

ACTIVITY Hold your baby outwards so their back is against your chest. Take them out into the garden to show them the trees or plants, tell them the names of the plants and see if they can grip a leaf in their hands. If you don't have a garden, do this while out on a walk. Take your little one out of their pram so they can see the shapes, colours and movement of the trees.

Week 15 Day 5

Your baby is soaking up everything you say at the moment, so remember to chat, chat, chat to them. And don't worry if you feel that you're repeating yourself; repetition is wonderful for your little one's learning and understanding.

ACTIVITY Every time you speak to someone on the phone, tell your baby who called and what they said. It's such a simple activity, but it will add to their vocabulary and also make them feel included, stimulated, engaged and entertained. If anything funny happened, tell your baby! They will love hearing the humour in your voice and sharing a laugh with your baby will make you feel more connected. For example, you could say, 'Silly Aunty Sophie forgot it was Granny's birthday . . . Uh oh, she's in trouble!'

FACT A study from the University of Bristol in the UK found that babies as young as four weeks old can understand and feel humour. Humour and the feeling of laughing alleviates stress, allows the expression of feelings and creates a bond between individuals.

FOOD FOR THOUGHT It won't be long before your baby is ready to start enjoying some puréed food. I love the weaning stage! I know it can be quite daunting at first but very quickly your baby will be happily eating toast for breakfast and fish pie for tea!

There is a big debate over when to start weaning. In 2001, the World Health Organisation (WHO) changed its advice. It said weaning should start at six months, not four months, as previously advised. This change is due not to babies' digestive systems being underdeveloped, but the WHO taking into consideration developing countries where contaminated water and a lack of sterilisation means that breastfeeding exclusively is best for the first six months.

By the age of six months, babies are able to enjoy and actually need the nutrients from meat, fish, dairy and carbohydrates. But they also need a few weeks for their digestive systems to get used to simple vegetable and fruit purées before being introduced to more complex food groups, which is one of the reasons I advise offering first tastes before six months.

Think today what you might need to buy before starting to wean. Do you have a long-sleeved bib, a bowl, a silicon baby spoon, highchair and blender?

16 Weeks Old

It's almost time for your baby's last set of vaccinations. After this, they won't need any vaccinations until they are twelve months old . . . hooray!

As before, they may be unsettled at night, or more clingy during the day. The side effects should only last a few days, so keep them as comfortable as possible with lots of TLC. They may want to feed little and often.

Just because your baby reacted to one vaccine doesn't mean they will have the same reaction the next time, so go in with an open mind.

TIP Don't forget to take their red book so your doctor can record the date the vaccinations were done.

FACT Your baby's posterior (back) fontanelle should have closed by now but their anterior (top) fontanelle will close anytime between now and two years old. They are the two soft spots on your little one's head where their skull plates meet. It is safe to gently touch their fontanelles if you want to feel them.

Week 16 Day 1

Nappy rash is something that can normally be prevented, by changing your little one's nappy regularly and making sure the area is clean and dry before putting a new one back on.

TIPS These are my top tips for preventing nappy rash:

- Change your baby's nappy at every feed time and as soon as they poo.
- Use tepid water and cotton pads or non-alcoholic and unscented baby wipes.
- Wipe from front to back on a girl.
- Don't just wipe your baby's nappy area if they are dirty. Always clean it even if they are just wet.
- Give your baby lots of time without nappies to air their bottom.
- Make sure their bottom is clean and dry before putting a nappy back on. Use a piece of tissue paper or specific bottom cloth to dab their bottom dry after using wipes or cotton wool and water to clean the area. You can also blow on their bottom to make sure it's dry. Babies think this is very funny!
- Use a little coconut oil after a dirty nappy to moisturise the skin. Coconut oil has great natural soothing properties and lets the skin breathe, unlike barrier creams. I don't recommend barrier creams, as they clog the skin.

Unfortunately, sometimes the acidity of your little one's poo will cause the skin to burn and get sore. This is usually if they have an upset tummy or after taking medicine, and it's something you can't prevent. Use all of the above tips and a barrier cream to help clear the rash as soon as possible.

Week 16 Day 2

The four-month sleep regression is talked about a lot, but I believe it is due to hunger and a sign that your baby is no longer satisfied with milk alone.

I recommend you increase the quantity of milk they are having during their daytime feeds, or begin weaning once they are over seventeen weeks old, have doubled their birth weight and are showing signs of being ready to wean.

Signs of being ready to wean include:

- Watching you eat
- Feeding for longer (if breastfed)
- Draining every bottle (if bottle fed)
- Wanting to be fed earlier than normal
- Chewing on their hands
- Able to support their head unaided

FACT Your baby's chubby cheeks are made of fat and muscle. They need cheek muscles to help them drink milk. The repetitive movements from drinking milk so often in the first few months keep the cheek muscles strong and looking rounder.

TIP If you have an upright bouncy chair, it's a nice place to start your baby weaning as they will feel comfortable and well supported in it. Once they are stronger and are able to sit up with support, they can move into a highchair.

Week 16 Day 3

FACT The first primary colour your baby can see is red. They are now starting to distinguish different shades of colours, which is very exciting!

ACTIVITY Hold your baby outwards so they can see all around. Walk around your house showing them different photographs or pictures you have on display. Tell them who is in each picture and when each photograph was taken. Your little one is soaking up all the names of the people you are talking about and their understanding is permanently developing. They will love seeing the patterns and shapes from a new perspective!

MINDFULNESS A baby might have been all you ever wanted – however, the reality is hard. Take a moment to stop and appreciate all you have. What have you got now that five years ago you dreamt of having?

TIP Whenever you go out, always take a spare top or jumper of your own in case your little one is sick on you! You will be so grateful if and when the time comes.

Week 16 Day 4

Reading one book a day exposes your baby to around 70,000 words each year!

I would advise choosing some books for your little one that have simple and repetitive text with clear and colourful illustrations. Start to create a little library that they will enjoy for years to come. Charity shops often have a great collection.

Your baby will enjoy hearing your voice, especially if there is a sing-song or rhyming rhythm to the words. I always choose books which I like reading so that I'm engaged in the story too!

FACT If you read just one story a day to your child, they will have read 1,825 by their fifth birthday.

ACTIVITY Choose a story book with lovely bold illustrations to show your baby. You don't have to read the words to enjoy the book. Simply point to different pictures on the page and tell them what it is; for example, 'Here's the sun, there's the tractor . . . ooh look, the frog is on the water,' etc.

The more things you point out to your baby, the more interested and focused they will be, making storytime last longer before they lose interest.

> 'There are many little ways to enlarge your child's world.
> Love of books is the best of all.'
> *Jacqueline Kennedy, former First Lady*

Week 16 Day 5

FACT Your baby is growing about 1–1.5cm each month!

ACTIVITY Try clapping your little one's hands. Lay your baby on a comfortable surface and hold both their hands as you do the movement, saying, 'Clap, clap, clap, your hands.' If they like the feeling and want you to do it again, sing this song at the same time:

If you're happy and you know it, clap your hands
If you're happy and you know it, clap your hands
If you're happy and you know it
And you really want to show it
If you're happy and you know it, clap your hands

Show your little one how you can also clap your hands together; they will like hearing the noise and with repetition over the next few weeks and months, they will start to copy you and clap their hands on their own. By saying 'clap, clap, clap', and singing the song at the same time, they will learn the connection between the word and the action.

Week 16 Day 6

Remember that there is no training to being a parent, so don't expect to know everything. Never be afraid to ask for help.

Find your tribe. Everyone has a different opinion so choose to listen to those who make sense to you and your baby.

FACT During their first three to six months, your little one's ears grow rapidly. However, the growth slows down after this point until they become an adult.

REMINDER Here is a reminder to take your monthly photo today of your baby alongside your chosen teddy bear. This is number four of your twelve photographs, which you can keep to document your little one's growth during their first year.

17 Weeks Old

Now that your little one is at an age where they might be starting their first tastes, I want to dedicate a whole page to choking.

Your baby will gag at times during their weaning journey.

It's important to understand the difference between gagging and choking and to stay calm so that your reaction doesn't panic them and make the situation worse.

FACT Gagging is loud and choking is quiet. If your child is coughing and making a noise, it means that air is passing through their airways. If your baby or child is silent and not making any noise, you need to react quickly to help them dislodge the obstruction.

Here are the steps to follow if you think your little one is choking (the below is for babies under the age of 1):

1. Shout for help.
2. Remove them from the highchair.
3. Sit or kneel and lay your baby over your forearm or thigh, face down, head lowered, supporting their head.
4. Give up to five sharp blows between the shoulder blades with the heel of your hand.
5. Turn your baby over and lay them on your thigh. Support their head and lower it.
6. Place two fingers in the middle of their chest below the nipples and give up to five chest thrusts. The aim is to relieve the choking with each thrust rather than give all five.
7. Call 999 if the object hasn't dislodged and keep alternating this cycle of back blows and chest thrusts until help arrives.

HOW TO Follow the link on this QR code to watch my thirty-second video on what to do if your baby chokes.

Week 17 Day 1

FOOD FOR THOUGHT Your baby might be ready to start weaning. If they aren't showing the signs just yet, you can still make and freeze some purées for when they do start.

For the first few weeks, until your baby is six months old, the only thing you should give them is fruit or vegetable purées, or baby rice mixed with breast or formula milk. You can adapt the basic recipe below for any vegetable.

I suggest cooking the fruit and vegetables on your hob. You can also steam the vegetables, but I find they don't purée quite as well.

Never add salt to a baby's purée – they should have no added salt until they are at least a year old.

I haven't included quantities below, as it depends whether you want to make individual portions or make a batch of purées and freeze them. You can freeze the purées in ice-cube trays so you defrost small quantities at a time. Transfer the cubes into a freezer bag when frozen and make sure you label each batch with the date. The food cubes can be kept in the freezer for up to three months.

Here is a recipe for your baby's first purée: Sweet Potato Purée.

1. Peel and chop the sweet potato into chunks and simmer in a little water until soft enough to purée.
2. Drain, keeping some of the water.
3. Blitz in the blender until you get a smooth consistency.
4. If it's still too thick, add some of the water or your baby's milk (formula or expressed) until you get the right consistency.

TIP Offer your little one their first taste at 5 p.m. so that there is plenty of awake time before bedtime in case your baby reacts to anything. If you have older children, I would feed your baby while you give them dinner. As long as the meal falls between 4–5 p.m., you can be flexible with timings to suit your family.

When starting your little one's weaning journey, offer one food at a time, so that you know if your baby has had a reaction to it. This could be in the form of an upset tummy, a rash on the skin or redness around the mouth. If you mix purées, you won't know what food sparked the reaction. Once they have had tastes of single foods without a reaction, you can start mixing tastes, such as strawberries and bananas or sweet potato and courgette.

If your baby has a mild food allergy that causes the odd loose nappy and eczema in contained places on the body, always talk to your GP before adjusting your child's diet. It is usually advised not to cut out the allergen completely, and to continue to give small quantities within other foods.

In some cases, you are advised to remove the food that is causing your baby upset for a few weeks and then reintroduce it slowly back into their diet. This break is often enough to let your baby's digestive system reset and they then tolerate the food in question.

It is important not to restrict the diet any more than necessary, because babies need nutrients from all food groups.

Seek medical help immediately if any part of your baby's body starts to swell.

FOOD FOR THOUGHT I find it best to make each food separately and freeze it individually so you can mix and match the fruit and vegetables easily and you don't end up with a big batch of the same combination. For example, you could defrost a cube of carrot with a cube of spinach one day, and the next day a cube of carrot with a cube of butternut squash. For more defrosting and reheating tips, see page 150.

Week 17 Day 3

If you haven't already, it's time to transition your baby out of their swaddle and into a sleeping bag. See page 121 for my advice on making this an easy transition.

FACT Most babies are born with blue-grey eyes but they will often change colour. If your baby's eye colour is going to change it will usually do so by six months old. Blue or light-coloured eyes will often change and go darker, whereas darker eyes will often stay the same.

ACTIVITY Use a ribbon to measure how long your baby is. Cut the ribbon to their length and add it to your memory box.

REMINDER This is your reminder to write a letter to your little one to add to their memory box. Include any developmental milestones, places you have visited and people you have met.

Week 17 Day 4

When you offer your baby their first tastes, make sure you are confident and smiling at them so they have your reassurance that this is a fun, new experience. If you chat to your little one, they are more likely to open their mouth and take the purée from the spoon.

FOOD FOR THOUGHT Defrost your frozen purée by taking out the cubes you want to use the night before and let them defrost slowly in a covered dish in your fridge.

Warm the vegetable or fruit purée in a small pan on the hob, and serve at room temperature.

To reheat purée I prefer to use a pan on the hob; however, if you are using a microwave make sure the food is piping hot and stir it well to avoid any hot spots occurring – then allow it to cool before serving to your baby so they don't burn their mouth.

Once the food has been heated, it cannot be refrozen or reheated and must be thrown away.

TIP While weaning, try not to give too many fruit purées at first; instead stick mainly to vegetables. This is so that your baby doesn't get too used to only sweet tastes and then refuse the savoury.

Week 17 Day 5

Is spoon-fed or baby-led weaning best?

I believe you should use both. I like to start spoon-feeding babies puréed foods so that they don't get frightened by choking. When they are six months old I start to offer finger food for babies to hold, suck, chew and explore while I make sure they are getting all the goodness and nutrients from what I am spooning in.

I like to know how much food a baby is eating. This is difficult when you are only giving finger foods as so much seems to end up on the floor! I also like to give warm, comforting meals to babies from six months old – fish pie and cottage pie purées, etc. I don't think babies get enough from baby-led weaning alone.

TIP Use your baby's milk (expressed breast or formula) to thin the purée if it's too thick. Use baby rice to thicken a purée that is too runny.

ACTIVITY Start encouraging your little one to play independently even from this age – just short periods at a time where you are able to do some tasks while they play within your reach. Lay them on a playmat or in their Moses basket, and prop up some high-contrast images for them to look at. Toys that dangle from the play gym fascinate babies and are a good way of holding their attention. Talk to them, and tell them how clever they are, so they have the security of knowing you are still in the room.

Week 17 Day 6

From this age I give babies a bed toy once they are out of a swaddle and sleeping in a sleeping bag.

Babies love the feeling of having something soft to hold and it's nice for them to have the comfort at bedtime of something with a familiar smell and feel.

If the toy is left in their cot, and only used at bedtimes, then the children look forward to jumping into bed so they get their comforter – bed becomes a happy place, not a punishment.

The toy also becomes a sleep aid. If the child associates their toy with sleep, then wherever you are – in the car, on a plane, in a different time zone – they automatically think of sleep when you give them it. I've often hidden a bed toy in a changing bag on a long plane journey and brought it out when it's time for baby to sleep – it works wonders!

Make sure the toy is made from soft, lightweight material and roughly the size of your hand. If you use a muslin as their comforter instead, tie a knot in the muslin so that it isn't long enough to wrap around them.

18 Weeks Old

Babies and older children go through periods of growth spurts. It is very possible your little one is having a growth spurt if they are sleeping for longer, hungrier and . . . growing! For tips on how to deal with this, see page 33.

FOOD FOR THOUGHT Now your baby has had a week of vegetables, you could try an occasional fruit-based treat, such as this Blueberry and Baby Rice Purée. You can adapt this recipe for other fruits, such as pear, apple, mango or peach. Bananas and avocados also make great fruit purées – they don't need cooking but you might need to thin them slightly with your baby's milk at first.

1. Simmer the blueberries in a little water for 1 minute, just to soften them, then blend until smooth.
2. Make up the baby rice as per instructions, using your baby's milk.
3. Mix the two together and serve.

TIP Once your baby is weaning, I always say you should feed the rainbow – that is, lots of different-coloured foods throughout the course of the week.

Week 18 Day 1

FACT Human babies are the only babies in the primate family that smile at their parents . . . Remember to keep smiling at your little one so they copy you back!

ACTIVITY Looking in a mirror with your baby is not only really fun but it can help your baby learn to focus and track images. Seeing their reflection helps social and emotional development as your little one interacts with you. Talk to them through the mirror and point to different parts of their body, naming their nose, ears, toes, etc.

TIP Once your baby has had a week of first tastes at 5 p.m., you can start to offer them a lunchtime purée at 11 a.m., as well as their teatime purée. At the 11 a.m. feed, offer half a milk feed so they're not starving. After a five-minute break, pop them in their chair and offer them some solids – as much as they are happy to take. Once they lose interest, they've had enough. Wind them, give them a twenty-minute break and then offer the rest of the milk feed.

ACTIVITY Playing music in the house will create a nice atmosphere and background noise for you and your baby and will help them play happily for longer without feeling that they have been abandoned!

ACTIVITY Encourage your baby to chuckle and interact with you by playing peekaboo games while they're in their bouncy chair. Use your hands or a muslin to cover your face and build excitement, then reveal yourself and say, 'Peekaboo – I see you!' Playing this game helps your baby understand that objects and events continue to exist, even when they cannot be seen, heard or touched. This is called object permanence.

TIP Once your little one has tried a type of food on its own, you can start to mix the purées with one another. For example, if your baby is fine with pear and potato purées separately, then mix them together! Sweet and savoury mixtures may sound unappetising to us but the potato brings a bit more substance and makes the meal less acidic for your baby.

Week 18 Day 3

There are a hundred reasons why it's great to read books to your baby. It improves their cognitive development, enhances their understanding of the world, encourages bonding, and of course has a hugely positive impact on their speech and language development.

You can buy baby books that include flaps for your little one to lift to see what's hiding underneath, and different textures on pages for them to feel. These provide a sensory experience alongside the language development.

ACTIVITY Say your little one's name throughout the day so that they begin to recognise it.

FACT Your baby's poo consists of all the food they have eaten that can't be digested or absorbed by their body. Therefore, it can change colour frequently.

TIP Offer your baby cooled boiled water in a bottle or a beaker with a soft teat alongside each purée. This will help aid digestion.

Week 18 Day 4

As your baby grows, their immune system strengthens and it won't be long before they're putting everything in their mouth as a way of exploring the world.

It's actually good to expose your baby to friendly and harmless germs, so try not to worry too much.

It is important to clean your little one's toys and equipment regularly, but without creating an environment that is so sterile that your baby cannot build up an immune system. Wipe their toys weekly or as needed with warm soapy water.

Most bouncy chairs have removable covers that you can put in the washing machine. Car seat covers also come off easily – just make sure you don't put them in the dryer as they will shrink! Always use a non-biological washing powder.

FACT Your baby will quadruple in size in the first two years. After this point, their growth will begin to slow down.

FOOD FOR THOUGHT Between now and six months of age, your little one is more likely to accept bitter-tasting foods.

Week 18 Day 5

ACTIVITY Sing 'Tommy Thumb' to your baby. Wriggle your thumb to emulate Tommy and then hide it as you say, 'Where are you?' When you sing, 'Here I am,' pop your thumb up.

Tommy Thumb, Tommy Thumb
Where are you?
Here I am, here I am
How do you do?

FOOD FOR THOUGHT If you are breastfeeding, milk production uses your body's fat reserves, protein, carbohydrates and minerals to give your baby everything they nutritionally need.

TIP Banana, papaya and avocado are my go-to foods in a hurry as they don't need any cooking. All you have to do is whizz them up in a blender and serve! Banana and avocado go really well together and can be a breakfast, lunch or dinner.

Week 18 Day 6

Something to remember: put yourself in your baby's shoes. When thinking about how to dress them for the weather, how do you feel? Have you got a big coat on, for example? Are your hands cold in the wind? By putting yourself in their shoes, it's a way of understanding why your baby might be unhappy. Maybe they are lying uncomfortably, or are too hot, cold, hungry or overtired.

TIP When dressing your baby, beware of buttons or bows on their back, which may make it uncomfortable for them when trying to sleep or in the car seat or pram.

FACT Research shows that picking up the pace when you are walking will actually boost your energy levels. Speed walking causes a rush of endorphins which can relieve stress, improve your sleep and boost your mental health. While out on a walk with your baby, try speed walking for intermittent periods.

19 Weeks Old

Eye contact is important for successful interaction and communication with your baby. Being face to face lets them see where the sounds you are saying are coming from and allows them to observe your facial expressions.

Try holding something up to your face such as a noisy rattle so that it brings their attention to your face.

ACTIVITY If you have been exercising consistently for several weeks now and are starting to plateau with your training, try upping the weights or doing more reps for each exercise.

So if you're exercising at home and have been doing an exercise like squats for thirty seconds then resting for thirty seconds before moving on to the next exercise, up the timer to forty seconds and just have a twenty-second rest.

HOW TO With the following exercises, aim for forty seconds, followed by twenty seconds of rest. Repeat each exercise two to five times.

- Deadlift to overhead press
- In and out squat jumps
- Weighted punches
- Curtsey lunges
- Bent-over rows

Week 19 Day 1

If your little one has been having a lunch and teatime purée for the past week, you can now introduce breakfast! Depending on your morning routines and structure, start the day as normal with a full milk feed. Roughly an hour later, offer breakfast fruit purée. You can add a little baby rice if you think the fruit purée is too sweet.

FACT Babies have 30,000 taste buds when they are born. This is three times as many as adults. They not only have taste buds on their tongues like us, but also on the sides and roofs of their mouths as well as on their tonsils and at the back of their throat.

TIP Save space in your nappy bag by putting one nappy sack into each nappy. That way you won't need to take the whole box or reel of nappy sacks.

Week 19 Day 2

Today, simply take two minutes to revisit the entry on page 57 and watch my baby CPR first aid video to refresh your memory in case of an emergency.

MINDFULNESS We hear music all the time, but it's usually in the background. Choose a time in the day when you won't be distracted, find a comfortable spot and listen to a piece of music properly. Focus on the instruments you can hear, the tones of the voice, and how the rise and fall of the music makes you feel.

Week 19 Day 3

ACTIVITY Have a shower with your baby so they get used to the feeling of the water and having the spray around their head and face. Give them confidence and reassurance by chatting to them and smiling, telling them how clever they are. Babies tend to enjoy this as they like the comfort of being held by you.

FACT Avocados contain unsaturated fats that support your baby's brain development and also gives them energy. Try your baby with a puréed avocado today. When they are older, you will be able to just mash the avocado with a fork so it creates a slightly lumpy texture.

MINDFULNESS Use the other half of the avocado to make yourself a face mask. Simply put the avocado, two tablespoons of honey and half a teaspoon of apple cider vinegar into a blender and blitz until smooth. Wash your face thoroughly and apply a thin layer of the mask while your skin is still damp. Leave on for fifteen minutes and then wash off.

Week 19 Day 4

FACT Your baby won't have full control over the muscles they use for swallowing, until they are around eighteen months old. Therefore it's common for little ones to dribble up until this age.

ACTIVITY When your little one is in the bath tonight, use your lips to make a 'brrrr' sound and see if they try to copy you. You can say things like 'the car goes brum brum', or 'brrrrr, the penguin is cold.' Your baby will enjoy listening to a new sound and watching how your lips move to make the sound.

FOOD FOR THOUGHT When you are cooking for yourself, get into the habit of making a little bit extra. For example, if you are cooking potato or vegetables, separate a few portions for your little one before you've added any salt or seasoning. Make them into a purée by blitzing and then freeze in small portions. By doing this you will create a stock of purées that you can defrost quickly for your baby's meals without having to cook every day. Remember not to refreeze any purées that have already been reheated.

Week 19 Day 5

Your baby's skill sets are developing quickly. Have you noticed them doing any of the following? I have divided the skills up into the five developmental categories so that you can see how your little one is progressing in all of the different areas. Don't worry if your little one can't do all of these things yet. Every baby goes at their own pace, though if you are concerned, please talk to a health professional.

Cognitive

- Able to track with their eyes as you move an object side to side
- Observes your face closely
- Responds to affection

Gross motor skills

- Uses their legs to support their weight when held on a surface
- Rolls

Fine motor skills

- Brings toys to their mouth
- Reaches for toys

Social and emotional skills

- Tries to copy your facial expressions
- Shows signs of frustration if bored or over-stimulated

Language and communication skills

- Laughs
- Babbles
- Turns when they hear voices

Week 19 Day 6

FACT Your baby's most sensitive touch receptors are in and around their mouth, which is why they put everything in their mouth.

ACTIVITY Put some teething toys in the baby bag so you always have something they can chew on when you're out and about.

TIP You can buy silicon teething necklaces that are safe for your little one to chew on. They can also be used when breastfeeding as a distraction – as your baby can touch and stroke them while feeding. The necklace can't be thrown on the floor, so it stays clean when you are out and about.

FOOD FOR THOUGHT If you haven't already, start experimenting with different food combinations for your little one to enjoy. Don't be scared of combining sweet and savoury flavours, as they often complement each other.

The reason I would like you to try mixing flavours early on is so that your baby enjoys their meals. For example, they will quickly get bored of eating a bowl of just puréed spinach, but spinach mixed with sweet potato is delicious.

20 Weeks Old

Are you thinking of returning to work yet? Maybe you have already done so or maybe you are planning to take a full year – or not return at all! Do whatever is right for you and your situation and try to make peace with it – there is no perfect solution.

If you are returning to work, the most important thing you can do for your baby is to make sure they are left in the care of someone who will love and nurture them and create a bond with them so that they're happy when you're not with them. Before you go back, have some induction days with the carer you have chosen for them so you can give your child a bit of extra time on the first few days and aren't rushing out the door. See below for some more tips on choosing childcare and settling your baby in.

Whatever childcare option you choose, make sure you organise it well before you need it; waiting lists can be very long! These are the main choices:

Nannies: A nanny will provide one-to-one care for your baby in their own home, with all the benefits that brings in terms of forming a close bond and maintaining your routine. Most nannies will also take on light housework tasks relating to your child, such as doing their washing, and are likely to be more flexible if you need occasional after-hours care. This is the gold-star option, but also the most expensive – and remember, if you hire a nanny, they are your employee, so they are entitled to holiday pay, a pension and sick pay, and you are responsible for paying their tax and National Insurance contributions.

Nurseries: A good nursery will provide plenty of stimulation and socialisation for your little one, and they generally work out as the cheaper option for childcare. However, if your baby is unwell, a nanny can still care for them at home, while a nursery will not accept them and you will still have to pay. You will also need to work round the nursery holidays and rigid drop-off/pick-up times.

Nanny share: If a friend or relative nearby also needs childcare, a nanny share could be a good option for you. A nanny will care for both children at the same time in one home. A positive is that your baby will be able to play with another child that they know and build a relationship with them. Nannies who work as a nanny share often charge a slightly higher hourly rate; however, once this is split between two families it typically works out cheaper than having your own nanny.

Childminder: A childminder works from their own home and cares for multiple children of different ages at the same time. It's more intimate than a nursery setting and it's significantly cheaper than hiring a nanny, but it does mean your baby will have to fit round the older children's routines.

Au pair: Having an au pair is a cost-effective method of childcare, but it is also a big commitment. Au pairs are usually young and inexperienced, so they may not have a huge level of knowledge when it comes to looking after a baby. As a host, you must provide a private room and meals for them, free of charge. They can work up to thirty hours per week, helping out with light housework and childcare, in return for 'pocket money'.

Grandparents/other relatives: If you are lucky enough to have relatives who are happy to care for your baby, this can be a great option – though the informal nature of the arrangement can bring its own challenges.

Week 20 Day 1

Now that you have left the newborn phase and your little one needs a bit more stimulation, here are my recommendations to help keep them entertained over the next few months:

- Tummy time water mat
- Jumperoo
- Teething toys
- Wooden activity cube
- Ball pool
- Play nest
- Highchair
- Floor mats to make playtime safe and comfortable

There are some amazing products on eBay, Vinted and Facebook Marketplace if you don't want to buy new – shop around to get the products for the best price in the newest condition. As these items are only in use for a few months, you could also speak to friends with little ones and see if they are willing to swap kit with you.

TIP If your baby is a bit wobbly in the jumperoo at first, you can tuck a towel in front of them to make it more comfortable by closing the gap.

ACTIVITY Buy a coloured helium balloon and tie one to your baby's leg while they are lying on a soft mat on the floor. Watch as they begin to kick and learn how the balloon moves as a result. Make sure the ribbon isn't tied too tight on your little one's leg and never leave them unattended.

ACTIVITY Why not try creating a sensory basket for your baby?

I find it really useful to keep a basket of sensory objects which your little one can explore. They should now be at the age where they are grasping things with their hands and bringing objects up to their mouth. The more stimulation you can offer your little one at this time, the happier and more content they will be. Baby toys are usually completely smooth, so by introducing different textures from around the home, it will enhance your baby's sensory curiosity and development.

Ideas for your sensory basket:

- Sponge
- Fabric such as wool and velvet
- Sensory foil blanket (can also be found in a first aid kit!)
- Rattle
- Sensory board book

Never leave your baby alone while they are playing with the contents of their sensory basket due to the risk of choking.

Week 20 Day 3

It's often the best time of day when you go into your baby's room in the morning after they've had a lovely long sleep, and they beam up at you and are so excited to see you – so remember to embrace those moments.

TIP A little morning ritual, whether it's having a cup of tea and a bottle of milk, or snuggling in bed for ten minutes, is precious.

FOOD FOR THOUGHT Coconut water is a great antioxidant and has many health benefits for you. It's a delicious and hydrating alternative to water and can be added to your smoothies.

I highly recommend buying some mini lolly moulds. They will be great for your teething baby, can make a brilliant snack and will help improve your little one's hand-eye coordination (see page 383).

If your baby is teething, Coconut Water Ice Lollies are a great way to cool and ease the pain on their gums. They can be offered from four months old. Simply add coconut water to mini lolly moulds and freeze until set. These are also nice for a child who is dehydrated through illness.

Week 20 Day 4

How are you? Remember that looking after yourself is part of looking after your baby.

Remember the old adage: 'Being a mother is the best reason to take good care of yourself.'

Every morning, promise yourself a treat that is just for you. It might be a bubble bath, watching an episode of your favourite TV programme, having half an hour in the garden, going on a run or buying some flowers. Self-care is so important.

MINDFULNESS Mindfulness is trying to focus on the present moment and enjoy everyday things we may rush.

FOOD FOR THOUGHT Eating fish is fantastic while you are breastfeeding because it is full of omega-3 fatty acids, but it's recommended that you only have two portions of oily fish (mackerel, sardines, salmon and trout) a week, due to mercury levels.

Week 20 Day 5

Your baby might start rolling onto their tummy at night-time as they become more mobile. As soon as they are able to get themselves into this position, it is perfectly safe for them to sleep this way. Continue to place your baby on their back when putting them in the cot.

If you've been using a baby bath seat, it might be nearly time to upgrade to a bath chair that's in the sitting position. If your little one is still a bit wobbly, use a flannel or small towel to support them in their new grown-up seat, until they are sitting up unaided.

You can purchase some fun bath toys for them to play with, but a set of plastic cups works equally well!

Once your little one is in a sitting position, they will have a different view at bathtime, which will open up the opportunity for more play.

ACTIVITY Say the 'Two Little Dicky Birds' nursery rhyme to your baby while they are in the bath. Use your fingers to pretend to be birds that fly away and come back, sitting on the edge of the bath.

Two little dicky birds sitting on a wall
One named Peter, one named Paul
Fly away Peter, fly away Paul
Come back Peter, come back Paul

Week 20 Day 6

As your little one isn't able to understand their emotions yet, you might find they are happy and excited one minute, then frustrated the next if an activity has stopped or they have become bored. Remember that they will also be sensitive to your emotions and will respond to things in a similar way to you. Therefore, if you are feeling anxious, the likelihood is your baby will be tearful or unsettled. This is another great reason to try to keep calm, even if you are upset.

MINDFULNESS Using your hand, touch your thumb onto your little finger and think about the number five. Take a deep breath and breathe out as you move your thumb onto the next finger, thinking about the number four. Repeat this for numbers three, two and finally number one – number one being when your thumb touches your palm. This quick mindfulness exercise will remove you from a stressful situation and stop you from reacting too quickly.

TIP When eating out with babies who are enjoying purées, I recommend taking homemade food with you. Insulated pots are great for keeping food warm in your baby bag until needed.

21 Weeks Old

What would you like your baby to remember about their first year, if they could?

Have a think today about the memories you'd like to make together. As the saying goes, the days are long but the years are short, and it's easy to get through each day without taking a breath and being present.

ACTIVITY Revisit the list you made on Week 10 Day 2 (see page 97) of the experiences that you would like your little one to have before their first birthday – are you now able to tick any off? Are there any things you would like to add? Think of small, achievable goals for yourself as well as for your baby.

FACT It's around this time that your baby's palmar grasp reflex will start to fade. This is the instinct that makes your baby instinctively grasp an object – such as your finger – if you place it in their palm. This reflex also causes their fingers to open if you stroke the back of their hand. The loss of this reflex is a sign that your baby is starting to use their hands more consciously.

Week 21 Day 1

FOOD FOR THOUGHT Did you know a watermelon is made up of 92 per cent water? I find most people love the taste of watermelon, which is great as they contain vitamins A, B6 and C plus antioxidants, potassium and amino acids. It's a really nice fresh juice to keep in the fridge – simply peel and deseed the watermelon and blitz in a blender until smooth.

TIP Sieve some of your watermelon juice and freeze it in mini ice lolly moulds as a refreshing accompaniment to one of your baby's meals or as a natural teething reliever for them.

REMINDER Here is a reminder to take your monthly photo today of your baby alongside your chosen teddy bear. This is number five of your twelve photographs, which you can keep to document your little one's growth during their first year.

Week 21 Day 2

Did you know that you are entitled to free dental treatment through the NHS until your baby is a year old?

I recommend that you book an appointment with your dentist soon as it's quite normal for your teeth to loosen during pregnancy.

FACT The acidity levels in your mouth increase due to hormonal changes while pregnant, which can cause cavities.

TIP When your baby is on their playmat, put them down in different positions so they get a new perspective during each play session. You can also move the toys around to encourage them to reach different areas. This will help develop their cognitive and motor skills.

Week 21 Day 3

A note about giving kiwi fruit to your baby for the first time.

FACT Babies and young children are at a higher risk of being allergic to kiwis than adults.

Mix a small amount of puréed kiwi with baby rice, so that the kiwi equates to just one-tenth of the portion.

Make sure there is at least one hour's wake window after giving your little one kiwi for the first time to make sure they don't have a reaction. Refer back to page 148 for more information about food allergies.

TIP If your little one isn't hungry enough at 7 a.m. to take a full feed, it's a sign that the overnight feed needs reducing or dropping completely. Reduce the amount of milk you give them by offering them the minimal amount of milk they need to settle back to sleep.

Week 21 Day 4

Babbling is one of the first stages of language development and generally begins at around five months old. Copy the noises your baby makes (this will also promote turn-taking). For example, if your baby says 'oooh', you say 'oooh' too, and see if they continue to say anything else! I love this stage; it's the sweetest when their eyes widen and they really feel they're having a conversation with you.

Around now, your little one also has the ability to copy sounds you make in certain situations. You might find they 'sing' when they play with an instrument or music is playing, or coo in a quiet voice at bedtime. When playing together, they might 'shout' when they get excited. Your baby will also now remember familiar books you read at bedtime and might become quieter when you snuggle up for a bedtime story.

ACTIVITY When in the bath tonight, soak a flannel in water and hold it over your baby's body so the water trickles over them. Sing 'Pitter Patter Raindrops':

I hear thunder, I hear thunder
Oh do you? Oh do you?
Pitter patter raindrops, pitter patter raindrops
I'm wet through, I'm wet through

Week 21 Day 5

I really encourage you to let your little one self-settle at nap times and at bedtime. It's never too late to start. I believe that having the ability to settle themselves to sleep happily in their bed is one of the best gifts you can give your baby.

If you always feed, hold or rock your baby to sleep, they will become dependent on this to settle and although it may be OK while they are still a baby, it will become tiresome for everyone if you have a toddler who can't go to sleep without you.

The earlier you teach them this skill, the easier it will be for them.

TIP Babies will probably have a wriggle and a little whinge for a few minutes while they work out how to fall asleep; this is normal so don't rush to pick them up. If they cry, put your hand on them and use a shhh-ing noise to soothe them. If this doesn't work, pick them up for a quick cuddle then put them back down. Repeat this until your baby falls asleep.

Week 21 Day 6

FACT Research shows that 78 per cent of mothers experience 'mum-guilt'.

You aren't alone if you are feeling this way.

Three things I would like you to remember on a daily basis:

- We were designed, as people, to raise children in communities with lots of help and support. If you are finding parenting difficult at the moment, it's perhaps because you are not getting enough support.
- Try not to put everyone else's needs in the family above your own. You are just as important and deserve a break and to have some fun.
- Get into the habit of focusing on what you are doing right, rather than what you feel you are doing wrong. Our brains have a tendency to focus on our wrongdoings.

22 Weeks Old

It's time to move on to Routine 4 – see pages 183 to 184.

Now that your baby is five months old, they should be able to drop their evening 4 p.m. nap. Make sure your baby sleeps in the afternoon until at least 3 p.m. so that they can stay awake until bedtime. If they wake before 3 p.m. try to resettle them, or you will have a tired baby who falls asleep during their bedtime feed.

This transition may take a couple of days for your little one to get used to, but persevere so that your nights don't begin to suffer. If your baby has too much sleep during the day then they will start to sleep less at night.

Routine 4 will vary depending on the stage of your baby's introduction to weaning; they may not be ready for three meals a day at the beginning of this routine change, but very quickly will be.

Routine 4

5 to 12 Months

At five months old, drop the early-evening 4 p.m. nap. Make sure baby sleeps in the afternoon until at least 3 p.m. so that they can stay awake until bedtime. If they wake before 3 p.m. try to resettle baby, otherwise you will have a tired baby who falls asleep during their bedtime feed.

At six months your baby should be having two naps a day and hopefully sleeping from 7 p.m. to 7 a.m. at night. The routine below will vary depending on the stage of your baby's introduction to weaning (see page 138). They may not be ready for three meals a day at the beginning of this routine change, but very quickly will be.

7 a.m. Hopefully your baby will wake anytime between 6.45 a.m. and 7.30 a.m. If they wake before 6.30 a.m., see if they can resettle themselves so that they don't get into a habit of waking early.

Change baby's nappy and give them a feed; they should be ravenous after all that sleeping! Incorporate some tummy time into their morning routine. Top and tail, moisturise and dress baby.

8 a.m. Breakfast purée.

9 a.m. Put baby down for a 1.5-hour nap. This nap gradually reduces over time. Each baby is different; some need two hours, others just an hour. As long as they are happy when they wake and can make it to 12.30–1 p.m. for their next nap then judge how much sleep they need.

11.30 a.m. Lunchtime purée with milk feed (this is the first milk feed to be dropped, once your baby is enjoying three meals a day, usually at seven months). Gradually reduce their milk feed and offer water instead.

1 p.m. Two-hour nap, in their cot if you are at home.

3 p.m. Milk feed.

5 p.m. Dinner purée.

6 p.m. Bath, tummy time and baby massage.

6.30 p.m. Milk, feed, wind, stories and cuddles.

7 p.m. Bedtime.

Week 22 Day 1

ACTIVITY It's a nice idea to find a local baby group to take your little one to. Most groups cater for children aged 0–5 years, are low cost and will give you the opportunity to meet new people. They are often held in village halls, community centres or churches.

FOOD FOR THOUGHT Try making a cup of peppermint tea. It has the following benefits:

- Freshens breath
- Relieves blocked sinuses
- Eases digestive problems
- Relieves headaches
- Improves sleep

REMINDER This is your reminder to write a letter to your little one to add to their memory box. Include any developmental milestones, places you have visited and people you have met.

Week 22 Day 2

By following my routine, your little one will get the right amount of sleep, meaning their awake time is happy and they are able to learn new skills and take in their surroundings.

A routine is there so that if you have a bad day – and this happens to everyone at times – or a day where you just have to go with the flow, you get back into the best rhythm for your baby the following morning.

Start the day fresh and wake your little one at the time stated on the routine. Follow the timings for the rest of the day and make sure you have a calm bedtime routine in the evening to set your baby up for a good night's sleep.

TIP I recommend you lower your cot base down to the next level now, as very soon your little one will start to move around a lot more and may be able to pull themselves up.

Week 22 Day 3

ACTIVITY Today, fold ten pieces of paper or card in half and make little footprint cards with your baby's feet.

You will be able to use these over the coming months to send to grandparents and friends as birthday or greeting cards. For an added cuteness overload, make your baby's footprints look like animals such as a bumblebee, ladybird or butterfly.

TIP Remember to put one of your cards in their memory box.

Week 22 Day 4

A note on early waking . . .

If your baby wakes between 5–6.30 a.m., try to resettle them so that they start the day closer to 7 a.m. with a lovely big feed. This enables you to continue on the usual routine. If you get your baby up and start the day at 5 a.m., they will want to nap by 7 a.m. and then your whole day's timing will be off, causing bedtime to be difficult. Try resettling your baby by tucking them in and using a white noise. If they are finding it difficult to go back to sleep, quietly offer them a small feed (as little as will satisfy them), and then wake them at 7–7.30 a.m. to start the day.

If your baby is having a dream feed, try increasing the amount they take so they are able to sleep until a reasonable time the next morning.

If your little one has started waking early after sleeping through before, it may be a sign they aren't getting enough food during the day to satisfy them all night. Try increasing the amount of purée you are giving them.

They could also be waking due to being cold, so make sure they are tucked in and snug with a blanket. Remember, we snuggle under a warm duvet.

TIP Make sure you have blackout blinds in place to stop the morning light waking them.

Week 22 Day 5

FACT Research suggests that cinnamon may protect brain cells.

FOOD FOR THOUGHT Try your baby with this Apple, Cinnamon and Raisin Compote with Weetabix recipe for a healthy start to the day.

1. Peel, core and slice an apple.
2. Simmer in a little water with the raisins and a sprinkle of cinnamon for 5 minutes, until soft enough to purée.
3. Drain, keeping some of the water.
4. Blitz in the blender until smooth, using some of the saved water to create the right consistency.
5. Add the compote to half a Weetabix which has been soaked in your baby's usual milk (expressed breast or formula).

TIP You can also add cinnamon to you and your little one's porridge, as another way of expanding their taste buds.

Week 22 Day 6

Your little one will go through periods of growth spurt, and it's common for one to happen at this time. Signs they are having a growth spurt will be if they are sleeping for longer, hungrier and . . . growing! For tips on how to deal with this, see page 33.

TIP When giving your baby their purée, open your mouth so your little one copies you and finds it easier to take the purée off the spoon.

ACTIVITY Puppets are a great toy at this age. You can use funny voices and your baby will be entranced by them. Let them reach out and touch the puppets. If you don't have puppets, choose a teddy from your little one's collection and give it a name. Talk to your baby through the teddy, using silly voices and moving it from side to side as though it's come to life!

If you do this regularly, your baby will learn the teddy's name. As they get older, it's a great way to encourage their language development, as the teddy can ask questions and start conversations as well as yourself.

23 Weeks Old

ACTIVITY Play the flying game. Carry your little one on their front with both hands holding them securely under their front and legs, and sway them gently from side to side while saying, 'Whoooosh!' Bend your knees and lower them as you bring them back to the middle then straighten up tall again as they 'fly' to the other side.

Do the movement nice and slowly to begin with to make sure your baby enjoys the sensation. This activity strengthens their head and neck muscles as they support their head.

MINDFULNESS If your to-do list feels endlessly long, set a timer for ten minutes and focus on one task only. Leave your phone in another room to avoid distraction. Let that one task have all of your attention for ten minutes until you hear the timer go off.

Week 23 Day 1

Now is a great time to start adding herbs and spices to your baby's purées. It will make purées more tasty and enhance your little one's taste buds. Introducing a wide variety of flavours now will make them more open to trying new tastes in the future.

It's safe to add herbs such as basil, dill, coriander, mint, thyme and rosemary, and spices such as turmeric, cinnamon and cumin, as well as ginger and garlic.

We add salt and pepper to our meals to make them more tasty; however, your baby's kidneys are not fully developed yet, therefore salt isn't safe for them. This is why I suggest using herbs and spices to season their meals instead.

FACT Fresh herbs aren't as strong as dried herbs; therefore, you can add more to your baby's purée than if you are using dried herbs.

TIP Add small amounts of herbs and spices so that they don't overpower your little one's dish.

Week 23 Day 2

FACT The most powerful phase of sleep is before midnight, when your body is restored physically, mentally and emotionally. Never feel guilty for having an early night!

ACTIVITY Fill a pan with lukewarm water and add a couple of waterproof toys that are small enough for your baby to grasp easily. Sit on the floor with your baby sitting supported between your legs, with their legs wrapped around the pan. Let them splash in the water and use their hands to grasp the toys, exploring their different senses. Adding lemon juice to the water will give them an additional smelling and tasting experience when they put the toys in their mouth.

TIP Place a hair band around your pack of baby wipes to stop more than one coming out at once.

MINDFULNESS You are in charge of being calm, even if everything around you isn't.

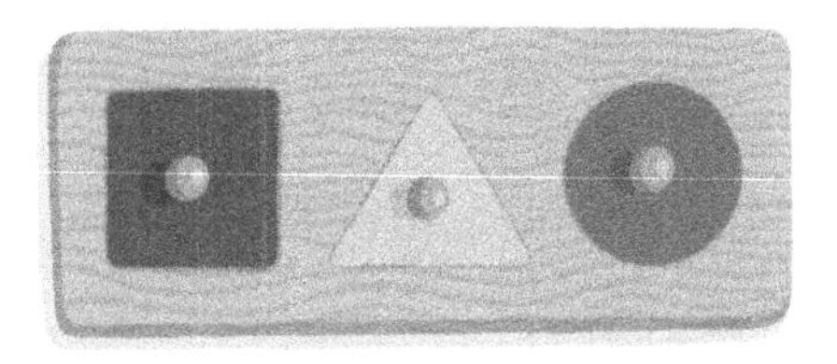

Week 23 Day 3

ACTIVITY Listen to 'The Happy Song' by Imogen Heap together. It's a song that was compiled to specifically appeal to babies and its magic formula helps to calm and fascinate your little one. Due to its simple melodies and rhythm that mirrors a baby's heartbeat, it somehow keeps hold of their attention. I would highly recommend adding it to your baby's playlist and using it in moments when your little one is fractious.

There is a video to accompany the song, which you can watch via YouTube – something you might want to do when your baby is a bit older.

FACT Asparagus is a great source of vitamin C and contains iron and fibre, making it a great immune-boosting food. Try your baby with some, cooked and blitzed in the blender with a little boiled water or milk.

TIP Boil the kettle each morning and fill a jug with water, letting the water cool. You can use this water throughout the day to offer to your baby alongside their purée. You can also add this water to your baby's purée if the consistency is too thick.

Week 23 Day 4

Your baby doesn't need loud, battery-operated toys to hold their attention. You will be amazed at how focused and intrigued they can be with something as simple as a loo roll tube.

ACTIVITY Cut loo roll tubes into 3–5cm-wide rings and place them on the floor. Let your little one explore the rings during tummy time. Roll up a blanket to use this as a support. Place the rolled-up blanket under your baby's chest and arms, giving their arms more freedom of movement to grasp and explore the rings.

By strengthening the muscles in their hands and fingers, they are improving their coordination. Watch your baby as they focus and persevere in trying to grasp and move the rings.

TIP Give them time to explore this activity before you jump in and help, as it's great for them to practise their problem-solving skills. Sometimes it's your natural instinct to try to help when you can see your little one is struggling with the task; however, trial and error is important for their development.

Week 23 Day 5

TIP During teething, your baby may become fussy while eating their purées. This is because their mouth is sore, so they may just want to chew on the spoon or a teething toy instead. Try a cool purée from the fridge to see if that's more comfortable for them and give them teething granules before offering them food.

ACTIVITY A super simple way of adding sensory play to your baby's daily routine is by washing their hands. Use a mild, bubbly soap that they can see, feel and smell on their hands. They will enjoy listening to the sound of the running water as it washes the bubbles away. When drying their hands with a towel, talk about pat, pat, patting them dry.

MINDFULNESS Instead of letting the thought of everyday tasks get you down, try to relax and be in the moment. Put some music on and have a little dance while you wash up or listen to a podcast while you fold the laundry.

Week 23 Day 6

FACT Your baby won't show a preference for using their right or left hand before they turn eighteen months.

ACTIVITY Wet a flannel and roll it up, then twist it into a circular lollipop shape. Place in a freezer bag and freeze for thirty minutes. Let your baby hold and chew this as a homemade teething toy that is cooling for their gums.

TIP Sit on the floor and prop up your baby facing outwards, either on your lap or in between your legs, so you are their support while they look out or play with a toy.

24 Weeks Old

Your little one's daytime naps are really important, as good sleep in the day brings great sleep at night.

If your baby is waking from their nap after half an hour or forty minutes, it doesn't mean they've had enough sleep. You have to help them link their sleep cycles. By following Routine 4, you will know whether your baby is getting enough sleep.

If your baby gets up too early, they will be unhappy and unsettled during their awake time. Help your baby settle back to sleep on their own by making sure they are comfortable and cosy. Think to yourself:

- Are they warm enough?
- Could they be hungry?
- Have they got wind?
- Is the room quiet and dark enough?
- Did they fall asleep by themselves?
- Are they relying on a dummy to fall asleep with and is this causing them to wake during a lighter sleep when it falls out?
- Are you using a white noise in the room and is it stopping during their nap?

TIP If your baby wakes early from a nap but is happy in their cot or pram, leave them to see if they fall back to sleep by themselves. If they are cross or crying, help them settle back to sleep using the same method you would at the beginning of their nap.

It may take a few days of you consistently resettling your baby when they wake early from a nap, but it will absolutely be worth it. Your baby's awake time will be much happier when they have proper naps.

Week 24 Day 1

If you are planning to return to work and you are considering an external setting such as a nursery or childminder, make sure you look round the premises in person (including outdoor facilities and food preparation areas), check out their Ofsted report, ask about the qualifications of the carer(s) and, if possible, speak to other parents whose children are looked after there. Think about things like whether it's easy to park at drop-off, and what their policy is if you are unavoidably late at pick-up.

Although waiting lists for nurseries can be very long, sometimes places come up at short notice so it's still worth putting your name down if you haven't already done so.

Keep in mind your little one needs to build up their familiarity with the place as well as relationships with the carer(s). This is much easier to do if you take them at least twice a week, even if only for a few hours at a time. If possible, I would avoid only booking them in once a week as I find children don't settle as easily.

Before you settle your little one into nursery or leave them with a childminder, make sure you discuss the following:

- Sleep habits
- Eating habits
- Medication
- Allergies

Ask how communication takes place as it can vary. Some settings have an online portal where they post updates throughout the day, whereas others may fill out a book instead.

If your little one is used to having a comforter and white noise at nap times, inform their childminder or key worker and make sure you pack them in their bag.

Week 24 Day 2

If you are planning to return to work and would prefer to have someone caring for your baby at your home, you might be considering a nanny or au pair. Having someone in your home is very personal; you need to be able to get on with them and be able to walk out the door knowing your child is in the best hands.

Leave plenty of time to search for the right nanny for you. Even if you are using an agency, check references personally. I always find calling previous families they have worked for is better than an email as you can chat about why they are leaving and if it was a positive experience etc. Ask to see their First Aid Certificate, an up-to-date DBS form, driving licence and any other qualifications.

During interviews, be open and discuss the job role in detail and what duties will be expected of the nanny. If you suspect there may be additional hours required, such as babysitting or travelling, be honest and gauge their reaction!

I would also suggest a trial day where you can let the candidate have more time playing with your baby before you make your decision.

Finally . . . trust your instincts! Gut feeling is very important.

Here are some questions you might ask a nanny in an interview:

- Why did you decide to become a nanny?
- Can you give me examples of how you would plan a day with the children?
- What are your hobbies outside of work?
- What are your views on discipline?
- Have you ever had to deal with an emergency situation?
- Do you enjoy cooking?
- What are your strengths/weaknesses as a nanny?
- Why are you leaving your previous position?
- Are you looking for a long-term position, or do you plan to go on and do something else in the future?

Week 24 Day 3

Being a parent is tiring.

Here are five instant energy fixes:

- A cold shower
- Not skipping breakfast
- A brisk walk
- Eating healthy snacks such as fruit and nuts
- A twenty-minute power nap while your little one sleeps

ACTIVITY Lay your baby on a comfortable surface and place ten toys around them in a circle. The toys should be just out of their reach to encourage them to stretch and reach out while on their front. This is a good activity to encourage your baby to start crawling. Watch as they learn to pivot around the circle to get to the toys they desire.

TIP Check your baby's car seat straps sit parallel to their shoulders when fastened. You may need to alter them as your little one is growing.

Week 24 Day 4

You may have noticed that your baby's legs appear 'bow-legged'. This is completely normal; their legs are formed this way to make the most of the space they have in the womb during pregnancy. It's good to let your baby push up from a surface as it desensitises the soles of their feet.

Bouncing your baby up and down is a fun motion for them and won't cause them to have bow legs. However, make sure they aren't putting weight on their legs for long periods of time at this age.

FACT Once your baby begins to stand and walk, new bone will grow and mould to support their weight.

ACTIVITY Prop your baby in the corner of an armchair or sofa and talk to them so they start to gain balance and pull themselves forward to try to engage with you. Remember never to leave your baby here, though, as they could easily topple forwards and onto the floor.

Week 24 Day 5

Start giving your little one a baby toothbrush to play with at bathtime. This lets them put it in their mouths on their own terms; you're not forcing the brush in, which could cause them to resist having their teeth brushed in the future.

TIP Keep a toothbrush by your changing station to give them if needed. I don't put any toothpaste on the toothbrush until after they've had their milk as I don't think minty milk would taste very nice!

Use a tiny smidge of baby toothpaste and brush their little teeth for as long as they are happy for you to do so. Talk about how you are brush, brush, brushing their teeth to distract them. You can even turn it into a song.

ACTIVITY Incorporate animal noises into your little one's games and activities, such as when reading a story. This will help provide the foundation for their speech and language development. Teach your baby the different sounds that animals make. Making animal sounds seems like such a simple activity, but it's a really engaging way of teaching your baby about the world. Next time you read a story, make sure to 'moo' like a cow, 'buzz' like a bee and 'neigh' like a horse.

Week 24 Day 6

The current guidelines state you should sterilise your baby's bottles until they are twelve months old. However, I usually sterilise until they are around six months old and then swap to just cleaning thoroughly with warm soapy water.

By six months old, babies start to pick things up and put them in their mouths, and it's good for them to build up their immune system.

TIP Keep a tub of bicarbonate of soda in your cupboard. It's amazingly effective at absorbing smells and you can use it in the following ways:

- If your baby is sick on the carpet or on soft furnishings, sprinkle bicarbonate of soda over the area and leave for fifteen minutes before vacuuming up.
- Mix a solution of bicarbonate of soda with water. Dip a sponge in the solution to wipe and clean sticky toys.
- You can add a scoop of bicarbonate of soda to your washing to brighten clothes.
- Sprinkle some bicarbonate of soda in the bottom of the nappy bin to deodorise any lingering smells.

Another reason to keep a tub of bicarbonate of soda in the cupboard is you can add it to your little one's bath water if they ever get nappy rash or chickenpox. The bicarbonate of soda will help take the sting away.

25 Weeks Old

Allowing your baby to socialise with other little ones of a similar age is important for their social and emotional development. It will spark their curiosity, even at this age when they don't interact with each other. It's great to get them used to other children making noises around them so they learn to be happy and comfortable in different settings.

ACTIVITY Organise a little baby play date at home, at a local park or in a soft play centre. Make sure you time the play date so it's not at a time when your little one usually naps. I find a short play date of up to an hour is enough for a baby of this age.

TIP Always try to make your bed in the morning. Getting into an unmade bed at the end of the day can increase your stress levels and subsequently affect how well you sleep at night.

Week 25 Day 1

ACTIVITY Lay your baby on a soft playmat or on your bed and lie down next to them. Read a story while lying next to each other so your little one feels you next to them and looks up to see the pictures.

TIP If your little one is suffering from dry skin, moisturise with coconut oil in the morning and at bedtime. This will really help. If you start to notice your baby's scalp is flaky or dry, coat their whole head in coconut oil after their bath and let it soak all night. Wash their hair in the morning to take away the greasiness. Do this by wrapping them in a towel, holding them over the sink and washing their hair without having to bathe them. Remember to support their head so they enjoy the sensory experience. If you tackle their dry scalp as soon as you see it, it will stop cradle cap forming.

MINDFULNESS Find a moment this evening to look up at the stars . . . take a few deep breaths and think of everything in life for which you are grateful.

Week 25 Day 2

FACT When your baby blows raspberries, it helps them build strength in their facial muscles. These muscles are important for their speech development as they get older.

ACTIVITY Blow raspberries on your little one's cheeks and neck. See if they like it. This is both a sensory touch and sound sensation for them and they can learn to copy you in the coming months.

TIP When your little one first sits in a highchair, they might lean forwards and look a little uncomfortable. Tuck a tea towel at the front for added comfort, security and support until they become stronger in their back and can sit unaided.

REMINDER Here is a reminder to take your monthly photo today of your baby alongside your chosen teddy bear. This is number six of your twelve photographs, which you can keep to document your little one's growth during their first year.

Week 25 Day 3

FACT Studies show that lavender oil relaxes the mind and body, therefore promoting deep sleep for everyone!

ACTIVITY Add a few drops of lavender oil to your baby's bath, to relax them and create a sensory experience.

TIP When your little one gets a cold or blocked nose, create a steam room in your bathroom by closing the door and running hot water in the bath. Once it's all hot and steamy, add cold water until it's 38°C, which is the ideal temperature for a baby's bath. Use a warm flannel to wash and draw down a blocked and snuffly nose.

MINDFULNESS Get into the habit of wishing other people happiness. During the day, think of someone you care about and make a random wish for them to be happy. Keep it to yourself that you have sent this positive intention and energy. If someone annoys you or you fall out with someone, do the same. This will boost your own happiness too.

FACT The brain development during the first eight years of your little one's life builds the foundation for their learning in the future.

Now that your baby is approaching six months old, I have put together eight milestones which you can tick off if your little one has accomplished them.

If they haven't reached all of them yet, I'm sure it's nothing to worry about, but it's a good idea to have a chat with your health visitor. Remember, every baby goes at their own pace.

1. Grips a toy
2. Rolls front to back
3. Reaches for a toy on a playmat
4. Moves arms and legs when excited
5. Recognises familiar faces
6. Interested in their own fingers and hands
7. Interested in watching others eat
8. Giggles and shrieks with excitement

Week 25 Day 5

If you haven't started weaning your baby yet, it's probably time to start!

Milk alone can no longer satisfy your baby and they now need additional nutrients from proteins, fruits and vegetables. Be sure to try a wide variety of flavours so it extends their taste palates.

FACT Breast milk and formula no longer contain enough of the nutrients your little one needs for their growth and brain development. The reason your baby's head is big compared to the rest of their body is because the majority of their development across the first year happens in their brain.

ACTIVITY Narrate your day: what are you doing today? Tell your baby who they will see, where and when they are going. All of this additional conversation will aid your little one's speech and language development.

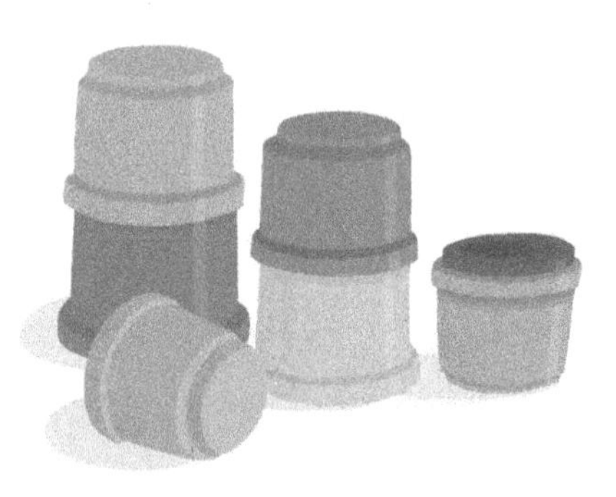

Week 25 Day 6

From today, as part of your morning routine, make up a beaker of water to offer your little one at mealtimes and throughout the day.

Take it with you in your baby bag when you are out and about, and let them hold it in their highchair so they learn to grip the handle and bring it up to their mouths themselves.

Until your little one is twelve months old, breastmilk or formula is still the most important source of nutrients for them so don't worry if they only take small sips of water. Some babies love to drink 140–170ml (5–6fl oz) of water a day and others will only manage a few sips – this is fine.

Some babies learn to drink from a beaker quicker than others, so if they don't like the feeling in their mouths, then I would use a bottle instead and try the beaker again in a few weeks. The most important thing is that weaning is a happy and stress-free time for your baby, and be assured that they will learn to take a beaker when they are ready.

TIP If you haven't already done so, you can move your little one into their own room now to allow them to sleep soundly without being disturbed.

26 Weeks Old

Lots of people ask me if they should warm their baby's purée and my answer is that I think most savoury purées are nicer warmed. At this important stage of weaning, you want to make your little one's food as appealing as possible so they enjoy the experience.

FACT Studies show that making a mess can boost your baby's brain. By letting your little one make a mess with their food, it will help them explore the different textures as they squash food with their hands and taste it. Using all of their senses helps them understand their surroundings.

ACTIVITY Try your baby with some finger food. Boil a few broccoli florets until they soften. Put them in front of your little one when they are sitting in their highchair and let them explore the touch, taste and smell. Encourage them to bring the food up to their mouths and tell them how clever they are – this will give them confidence. They will probably only suck bits of it, so remember that they will still need their purée alongside the finger food.

TIP Your baby is more likely to explore food when they are sitting in their highchair. Always sit with your baby while they eat. If you have to do something away from the table, make sure your baby is facing you so you can see them. Remember that choking can be silent so you wouldn't necessarily hear or know if your little one choked unless you can see them (see page 146).

Week 26 Day 1

Today I wanted to share what to do if your little one has a fever.

A fever is the body's natural response to fighting an infection, for example after having vaccinations, suffering from chickenpox, earache, coughs, colds or tonsillitis.

As a general rule, a baby with a temperature above 38°C is classed as having a temperature.

TIP Each child has a slightly different normal/base temperature, some being 36.4°C and others 37°C, and those with a slightly lower normal temperature will feel the effects of a temperature as low as 37.8°C. Take your baby's temperature occasionally when they aren't ill to see what constitutes a normal reading for them. This helps you judge how hot they are when they are unwell.

When you take your child's temperature, take readings from both ears. Don't take it just after a bath or if your baby has been wrapped in a blanket; briefly wait for them to cool naturally.

What to do if your child gets a temperature:

- Use baby ibuprofen (always follow the instructions on the packet).
- Keep a thin layer of clothing on them.
- Offer lots of fluids and snacks.
- Use a damp sponge or cloth with tepid water to cool their forehead and neck.
- Check their temperature every four hours through the night to make sure it hasn't risen.
- If it is only slightly above average, give them a bath as normal in the evening. Don't run a cold bath as this can send their body into shock – run the bath at 37°C. If your baby's temperature is above 38.5°C they will probably not feel like having a bath.
- Seek medical advice if your baby has a temperature of over 39°C, has a rash, is showing signs of dehydration or has had a temperature for longer than forty-eight hours.

Week 26 Day 2

Now that your baby is six months old, as long as they have had a couple of weeks' introduction to fruit and vegetables, they can now have meat, fish, lentils and dairy. This means their meals taste delicious and they can really enjoy their food.

FACT Your baby cannot have honey until they are twelve months old. This is because it may contain a bacteria called Clostridium botulinum, which a baby's digestive system can't cope with. It can cause a potentially rare but life-threatening illness.

Remember that just because you don't like a certain taste it doesn't mean your baby won't. For example, I really don't like the taste or smell of papaya, but I always give it to the babies and they usually love it.

Your baby can now also have eggs. I personally wait until they are ten months to give them scrambled and boiled eggs; however, they can have eggs well cooked through before then, such as omelette strips.

You will find their meal variety increases from now on, largely because they can have yoghurt and cheese . . . hooray!

If you notice your baby's eyes start to wander in different directions when they concentrate on a task, I would mention it to your health visitor. It's normal up to around six months for them to do this as their eyes strengthen; however, if you notice they are still doing it now then it's worth getting it checked out.

FACT Oats contain protein and fibre, which help keep your little one's heart and brain arteries clear.

FOOD FOR THOUGHT Porridge is a delicious and filling breakfast and can be brightened up by adding fruit purées. The baby porridge you can buy in shops is the same as normal porridge, but it is ground to a much finer consistency to make it smoother and easier to digest for your little one. You are paying a premium for them to do this and it takes two seconds to make your own.

To make your own baby porridge, blitz some oats in a blender and store in an airtight container. Add warm milk when ready to serve.

Now that your little one is enjoying a wider variety of food, they are able to eat the same as you. So if they are having a delicious bowl of porridge for breakfast, why don't you do the same? It's a great habit to get into as you will save both money and time by sharing the same meals.

Week 26 Day 4

ACTIVITY Find a photo of yourself at the same age as your baby is now and take a photo of your baby in the same pose and setting. You might want to dress them in similar clothes. It's fun to see any similarities or resemblance between you both.

TIP Whenever possible I like to offer babies fresh food which I have cooked. However, I know this isn't always possible. The food pouches available in shops are very handy to put in the baby bag when you're out and about. I advise choosing organic fruit and vegetable combinations as I don't like the idea of meat in a pouch that doesn't have to be stored in a fridge.

REMINDER This is your reminder to write a letter to your little one to add to their memory box. This month, include photographs of your baby with people they have met.

Week 26 Day 5

At six months old, it's time to move on to stage two formula if you are formula feeding your little one. Both stage one and two are very similar; however, stage two is slightly more filling and has a higher iron content.

FACT Finger food is a good way for babies to practise their pincer grip.

Here are some finger food ideas for you to give alongside your little one's main meal: avocado, broccoli, omelette slices (well cooked), toast, pear, boiled skinless potatoes, cereal, peas, strawberries, pasta, grated cheese, mango, raspberries.

If you can, cut the food into strips so that it is easier for your baby to hold and suck on.

If you are worried about choking, revisit page 146.

TIP Weaning is a messy experience. Try not to wipe your baby's face or hands too often and let them explore the different tastes and textures with their fingers. Wipe them at the end rather than constantly during their meal. A long-sleeved bib is invaluable at this stage!

Week 26 Day 6

Your baby may be going through another growth spurt. This could last for a few days so let your baby have a little extra sleep at their naptimes if they need it, and go with their increased appetite (see page 33).

FACT Natural yoghurt is a healthy snack choice for your baby. It's a good source of protein and contains calcium, which promotes strong bones and teeth. The live cultures also help support a healthy gut.

Yoghurt with fruit is one of my go-to desserts for babies this age. Greek yoghurt is thicker in consistency and easier to eat as it's less likely to slide off the spoon.

TIP Not all yoghurt is suitable for babies. Choose yoghurt that lists 'whole milk' as the first ingredient. Always avoid yoghurt made from raw milk, as this can contain bacteria such as salmonella and listeria. There are lots of yoghurts marketed for children but it's best to avoid any that contain added sugars at this stage, so check the labels carefully.

27 Weeks Old

Using a meal planner is a really helpful tool to see how varied your little one's diet is. By seeing the full week ahead in front of you, you will be able to keep track of how many times they are having the same meal and avoid too much repetition. It also allows you to see what ingredients you will need so that foods aren't going to waste.

Your baby needs food from each of the four groups below:

- Healthy fats will meet your baby's high energy needs. It's important to offer them full-fat food and to always avoid low-fat substitutes. Babies need oils and fats to increase their calorie intake, which helps them grow and their brain to develop. Your baby will get their fats from: yoghurt, cheese, butter, cow's milk in cooking, eggs, oily fish and nut butters. (See advice on cow's milk protein allergy on page 240.)
- Fruit and vegetables are packed with antioxidants, vitamins and fibre, and provide your little one with energy. The more colourful your baby's range of fruit and vegetables is, the better.
- Protein helps maintain a healthy immune system. It's an important nutrient that provides essential amino acids that will help your baby grow properly. Your baby will get their protein from: chicken, turkey, lean red meat, white fish, beans, lentils and tofu.
- Carbohydrates contain a variety of minerals and vitamins which are essential for your growing baby. Your baby will get their carbohydrates from: potatoes, barley, oats, sweet potato, pasta, bread and baby rice.

Week 27 Day 1

Your baby will love being able to sit; it gives them a different perspective on the world, rather than just lying down. Sitting up unaided usually happens between six and nine months old, although you can stop them becoming frustrated beforehand by using a seat aid.

To be able to sit up, your baby must be able to support their head and have enough strength in their body. Tummy time will help strengthen their back and neck muscles, which will help them when learning to sit up.

At first your baby may get their balance by leaning forward and using their arms to support them. Having a playmat or a soft surface will cushion your little one in case they topple – which could be to the side, forwards or backwards.

TIP Even when your baby is confidently sitting up on their own, always pop a pillow or something soft behind them in case they lose their balance and topple over.

As soon as your baby shows signs of sitting up, you need to lower the base of their cot if you haven't already. Once they can sit up, they can pull themselves up and would be able to fall over the side if the base is too high.

Week 27 Day 2

FACT Exposing your little one to a wide range of tastes will help them grow up to be less fussy. Research suggests that if your baby learns to enjoy foods within a certain category, such as vegetables, they will desensitise themselves to other foods within the same group.

ACTIVITY Start the 100-taste challenge.

As you know, I believe it is really important to introduce your baby to a huge range of tastes, textures and flavours in the first year so that they expand their taste palate and accept all the amazing foods the world has to offer.

Having weaned countless babies myself, I know there is a taste window where babies are a lot more likely to accept a food, which is why I have created a '100 foods in the first year' challenge. Follow the link on this QR code to find the list. Tick off the foods your little one tries and get inspiration from the recipes in this book.

Please note that the food on the taste challenge doesn't need to be tasted in numerical order and can be part of a meal rather than tasted on their own.

Week 27 Day 3

FACT Over the next nine months, it's vital that your baby's feet are able to grow naturally, so avoid tight socks or shoes.

ACTIVITY Now your baby is over six months old, make another print of your baby's footprints on an A4 or A5 piece of paper. Add this poem and frame for a nice keepsake:

Two little feet with ten tiny toes
Isn't it strange, how quickly time goes?
Footprints so small, but this will not last
You change each day, you'll grow so fast
These two little footprints will help me recall
How little you were when your feet were so small

Week 27 Day 4

FACT Babies under the age of one should have less than 1 gram of salt per day. As you know, your little one can't have salt added to their meals, but this poses a problem if you want to use stock in your baby's recipes, as instant stock cubes and tubs of ready-made stock are both full of salt. It might sound time-consuming to make your own salt-free stock; however, I'm going to show you just how easy it is to make in batches so you have plenty for the weeks ahead.

ACTIVITY Make a vegetable and chicken stock, and two batches of sauce: one cheese and one tomato. Freeze in cubes and pop them into freezer bags. This will help add flavour to your baby's food.

FOOD FOR THOUGHT Homemade Chicken Stock is packed with protein, vitamins and minerals and the amino acids and collagen support the immune system. Try making your own.

Ingredients
Chicken carcass
1 onion, chopped
1 leek, chopped
1 celery, chopped
1 clove of garlic, crushed
1 large carrot, peeled and chopped
A handful of parsley, chopped
1 bay leaf
Freshly ground black pepper

1. Put everything into one large pan, add enough water to cover the chicken carcass and simmer for 5–6 hours on a low heat with the lid on.
2. Allow to cool.
3. Strain the stock and divide into portions to freeze.

Week 27 Day 5

TIP We don't get enough vitamin D from food alone, so it's important that children under the age of five take a daily vitamin D supplement. If your baby is still drinking formula, you don't need to give this until they move on to cow's milk.

FOOD FOR THOUGHT Once your baby starts weaning you will see a variety of colours and textures in their nappies. Sometimes food travels through the digestive system so quickly that it doesn't break down. In particular, look out for grapes, raisins and sweet-corn!

ACTIVITY Lay on the floor, on your back, with your knees bent at a ninety-degree angle. Rest your baby with their tummy lying against your shins. Hold your baby under their arms to stabilise them while you rock back and forth, making a fun noise.

This exercise is great for your muscle strength and balance, as well as being a fun activity for your baby.

Week 27 Day 6

FACT Babies aged between six and eight months old learn to suck from a straw much quicker than an older toddler. This is because they have a natural sucking reflex and so don't have to be taught – it comes naturally!

ACTIVITY Give your baby a beaker that has an inbuilt silicon straw so they can master this skill now and won't lose it later.

FOOD FOR THOUGHT Make my super easy Teething Biscuits recipe for your little one. They make a great finger food.

Ingredients
200g oats
1 banana
2 teaspoons cinnamon
2 tablespoons coconut oil
1 apple

1. Preheat the oven to 180°C .
2. Put the oats in a blender and blitz for a few seconds.
3. Add the banana, the cinnamon and coconut oil.
4. Peel and chop the apple, and add to the blender, along with 2 tablespoons of water. Blitz until smooth.
5. Roll the mixture into sausage shapes (it will be quite gloopy) and place on a lined baking tray. Bake for 20 minutes.
6. Once the biscuits have cooled, store in an airtight container and freeze, or use within five days.

28 Weeks Old

FACT Omega-3 is an essential fatty acid which can only be consumed through food, oily fish in particular. It can also be found in eggs, edamame beans and sesame seeds. Omega-3 provides overall health benefits for your baby's body and keeps the immune system working as it should.

Four ways to add Omega 3 into your little one's diet:

- Scrambled eggs with cooked salmon
- Trout, cream cheese and broccoli purée
- Mackerel and avocado on toast as a finger food
- Omelette strips as a finger food

ACTIVITY Sing 'Round and Round the Garden' to your baby while using your finger to do a circular motion on their arm or leg. Using your touch while singing adds to their sensory and learning development.

Round and round the garden
Like a teddy bear;
One step, two step,
Tickle you under there!

Some babies like the feeling of being tickled, but others don't! So be led by them if you think they would enjoy a little tickle at the end of this rhyme.

Week 28 Day 1

ACTIVITY Try making homemade sensory bottles. Your little one will love the different noises they make when they shake them. You will need some clear, plastic bottles with a secure lid. Fill them with different substances that will create visual effects or fun sounds, such as:

- Blue food colouring and washing-up liquid to make bubbles when you shake
- Lentils to make a fun noise!
- Silver glitter in water for a bit of magical sparkle
- Coloured rice (put a few drops of food colouring into a freezer bag of uncooked rice, shake to cover then leave to dry for an hour or so)
- Red food colouring and glitter
- Some colourful pompoms

FOOD FOR THOUGHT Now that your little one is six months old, you can use cow's milk in meals, instead of using their formula or breastmilk, to make the purées a thinner consistency (see allergy advice on page 148). Please note that until your baby turns one, their milk feeds should still only be formula or breastmilk.

Week 28 Day 2

If your little one is struggling to have long naps as per the routine, re-settle them when they wake. They will quickly learn to link their sleep cycles. If you have tried the above for a few days and it isn't working, put a chair next to your baby's cot and sit with them until they fall asleep. You can put your hand on them or stroke their face but try to avoid picking them up or holding them until they fall asleep. Once you have successfully done this for a few days, try only sitting next to them for a minute or so. You want to gradually reduce the time you are there and move further away from the cot while your baby is awake, so that they learn to put themselves to sleep calmly.

TIP Your little one should be enjoying two naps per day. Their afternoon nap is more important than their morning one, so if you start to notice them finding it harder to settle for their afternoon nap, make their morning one slightly shorter.

Week 28 Day 3

FACT Your little one should never wear a coat or a snowsuit while they are in their car seat. This is to stop the harness being able to slip off your baby's shoulders if you were to crash.

TIP Keep a blanket in the car to tuck in over your little one after they have been strapped in. This will keep them both snug and safe.

ACTIVITY In the bath tonight, light a candle and listen to some relaxing music. Focus on three things in your life that you love. Take some deep breaths and smile while thinking about how they make you feel.

'When you focus on the good, the good gets better.'
Esther Hicks, inspirational speaker

Week 28 Day 4

200 days with your little one!

Today let's think about your own childhood and how it can help shape your baby's upbringing. What do you love about how you were brought up, and what would you change about how your parents parented you?

Draw on these experiences to make positive changes. You are in control of a new little life and you are able to stop any negative patterns recurring.

My tip to you would be to always put them first, not by giving them everything but by sacrificing things yourself. They will look back as adults and thank you so much for it.

'The way you speak to your child is their inner voice.'
Peggy O'Mara, former editor of Mothering *magazine*

Week 28 Day 5

FACT Your baby will enjoy feeling the texture of food in their hands. This is how they will learn about food, how it looks, smells, feels and tastes.

Today is all about how to serve finger food to your little one safely.

When thinking about whether you need to chop your baby's food into smaller pieces, consider its size and shape. Small, round, firm and slippery foods are more likely to get stuck. Examples of this are grapes, blueberries and tomatoes.

Remember that food with an outer skin is trickier for your baby to chew and digest, which is why you must always cut these types of foods up into pieces that are small enough so that if they were swallowed whole, they would pass through the airways.

Here are five safe ways to offer popular finger foods:

- Peel the skin off a cucumber before giving it to your baby in strips to hold.
- Cook vegetables to make them softer.
- Squish blueberries so they aren't round in shape.
- Aways cut grapes lengthways into four segments.
- When you are cutting food into strips for your little one to hold, such as meat and toast, make sure the width of the strip is roughly the same size as your finger.

TIP By giving your little one finger food to explore, it will stop them wanting to reach for the spoon you are using for their purée, which makes it easier for you to feed them. The finger food keeps them occupied and prevents them from getting bored or frustrated in their highchair during mealtimes.

Week 28 Day 6

Unless your baby suffers from allergies or there is a family history, it is now thought best to introduce your baby to nuts sooner rather than later, or at least before they are a year old.

Evidence shows that a delayed introduction to nuts may increase the risk of developing an allergy to them. If your baby does suffer from allergies, talk to your doctor about the best time to introduce nuts. (For more on food allergies, see page 148.)

TIP I recommend adding almond and peanut butter to some of your baby's meals. Here are some more ideas to introduce nuts into your baby's diet:

- Nut butters in porridge or on toast for breakfast
- Peanut butter on a rice cake or banana as a snack
- Chicken with peanut butter and rice for tea

29 Weeks Old

ACTIVITY When you're on a walk and you see something interesting . . . a horse in a field, or a digger working on a house, for example, lift your baby out of their pram so they can see from your perspective. Remember they're a lot lower down than you. Point out what you can both see and hear and talk to them about what it is.

TIP Now that your baby is becoming more mobile, make sure you always put them down somewhere safe and never leave them on a bed, sofa, changing table or at any height from which they can fall. A fall can happen in a flash.

FACT You might think that your baby is just eating their breakfast, but in fact there are eight senses that are working together while they are eating:

- Tactile (the touch/texture of the food)
- Auditory (sound)
- Visual (sight)
- Gustatory (taste)
- Olfactory (smell)
- Proprioception (bringing food up to their mouths)
- Interception (listening to their body and realising they are hungry)
- Vestibular (balance)

Week 29 Day 1

FACT On average, parents spend around £6,000 on their baby during the first year!

TIP You don't have to spend a lot of money to buy good products for your little one. There are some amazing baby items on eBay and Facebook Marketplace. You can buy everything for a baby, including cots, prams, baby baths, clothes etc. Shop around to get the products for the best price in the newest condition. You can also sell things once you no longer need them and borrow from friends.

ACTIVITY Do a toy swap with a friend. Pack up a few overused toys and swap with a friend who has a similar-aged baby for a month. You will save money and your little one will benefit from playing with new toys. It will also stop boredom and will enable new learning experiences through different toys.

Week 29 Day 2

What makes a happy baby? I think about this all the time.

Here is a list of what I feel makes a happy and thriving baby:

- They feel loved
- They are well fed
- They are well rested
- They are aware of a routine and continuity in their daily life
- They are given boundaries
- They live in a safe environment
- They are valued as part of a family
- They are shown kindness by those around them
- They are surrounded by humour
- They are given time and attention
- They are able to explore the outdoors
- They are interested in the world around them

None of the above involves expensive gifts or exotic holidays. No one single thing results in a child's happiness; it comes from having a sense of stability and being able to rely on the adults in their lives. These are the things that help to create a happy and thriving baby, toddler, child and then eventually young adult.

Week 29 Day 3

A calm night-time routine will help bedtime be a happy time.

TIP When you put your baby to bed, spend a few seconds cuddling them and saying, 'Night night, shhh, have a lovely sleep.' Once they are in their cot, smile at them and stroke their face or tummy for a while so they see you are happy, giving them the security that nothing bad is going to happen. Remember that your little one looks to you for reassurance.

ACTIVITY Your baby will love musical toys and by exposing them to musical instruments now, it will help to enhance their gross and fine motor skills, and speech and language development. Try getting them to copy you with a rhythmic beat by shaking an instrument. If you don't have any instruments, an upside-down pan and a wooden spoon works great as a drum.

Week 29 Day 4

ACTIVITY Make a treasure basket with objects from around the house. It's a brilliant sensory activity and helps your baby touch and feel different textures. Collect things like: a wooden spoon, ribbons, a small sieve, a lemon, something shiny, a cone from the garden, a sponge etc., and pop them in a shallow basket or box. The idea of a treasure basket is not to have plastic in it, as plastic is all the same texture – shiny and smooth. Bring the basket out for your baby and put it away again when the play has ended so they're excited each time it comes out. When your baby is exploring the basket, prop them up with some pillows around them in case they wobble. This activity should always be supervised.

REMINDER Here is a reminder to take your monthly photo today of your baby alongside your chosen teddy bear. This is number seven of your twelve photographs, which you can keep to document your little one's growth during their first year.

Week 29 Day 5

FACT Some baby wipes contain plastic and therefore are not biodegradable.

TIP Small cotton flannels that you can soak with warm water are much nicer and better for the environment for wiping your baby's hands and face after mealtimes. Fill a lidded airtight container with the cotton flannels and keep it near your sink. You can wash and reuse these. It's softer on your little one's face and they much prefer warm water instead of a cold baby wipe.

You can also fill your airtight container with water and a few drops of essential oils for the flannels to soak in, for added skin nourishment and a sensory experience.

FOOD FOR THOUGHT Avocado and banana blended together is a tasty, creamy treat for your little one. You can either spoon feed it to them or spread it on some toast and offer it as finger food.

Week 29 Day 6

FACT It can take up to two years for your iron to return to pre-pregnancy levels so keep eating red meat, apricots, green vegetables and eggs.

FOOD FOR THOUGHT Beef Stew and Dumplings is a recipe that both you and your baby can enjoy, plus it is a great way to boost your iron levels. This recipe serves six.

Ingredients
1kg beef braising steak, diced into cubes
2 tablespoons plain flour
3 tablespoons olive oil
1 large onion or 8 small shallots, peeled and chopped
3 carrots, peeled and diced
500ml unsalted beef stock
175g self-raising flour
75g shredded suet
A large handful of parsley, chopped

1. Preheat the oven to 120°C.
2. Coat the beef in plain flour and fry in a pan with a little oil until browned on the outside – this locks in the flavour of the beef.
3. Add the onion, carrots and beef stock and stir.
4. Cover with a lid and cook in the oven on a low heat for 2 hours until the beef is tender.
5. To make the dumplings, mix the self-raising flour, suet and chopped parsley with a little cold water to bind together. Use your hands to form them into small balls. Place the dumplings on top of the stew and cook with the lid off, on a higher heat of 180°C for 30 minutes until they are a lovely golden colour.
6. Blitz your baby's portion in a blender and add water until you reach the right consistency for your little one.

FOOD FOR THOUGHT If you are now giving your baby cow's milk mixed with food, watch to see how they react to it: an allergy to cow's milk is the most common childhood allergy, although 80 per cent of children will outgrow it by the time they reach school. The problem is that it affects babies in different ways and so is often hard for doctors to diagnose.

Green and/or stringy stools might indicate cow's milk protein allergy (CMPA), but not always. Other symptoms can include not putting on weight; vomiting; eczema that doesn't improve with treatment; tummy cramps and crying after a feed; red and blotchy skin around the eyes; a runny nose and congestion. Your baby may have one or a number of these.

From experience I can tell you that diagnosing a CMPA baby isn't easy. When you go to your GP and say your baby has green pooey nappies, is sick after feeds, and cries a lot they will often tell you that is what babies do! Be prepared for this and make the point that you know your baby and they seem unhappy for a reason.

If you are bottle feeding your baby, your GP will be able to prescribe formula where the milk proteins are broken down, making them easier to digest. When babies are prescribed specialist formula milk, they will often refuse it as the taste isn't as pleasant. This is more common in babies who are over twelve weeks old.

Try adding a few drops of alcohol-free vanilla essence to the milk once it's made up. And then once they are happily taking the milk consistently, you can start to reduce the vanilla essence and gradually stop adding it.

If you are breastfeeding your baby, you may have to adopt a dairy-free diet yourself, depending on your baby's sensitivity, as the cow's milk protein will carry through into your milk. This can be daunting but there are so many great dairy alternatives available in supermarkets now that it's not as hard as you think.

Week 30 Day 1

ACTIVITY Sign up to your local library. Not only will you be able to choose some fun books to enjoy at home together, it's also a lovely environment to sit in and make new friends. Most libraries hold baby groups and classes for little ones aged 0–5 years.

TIP Always check on your baby at night before you go to bed. Don't rely on looking at a monitor, as although many of them display the room temperature, you can't feel how warm or cool your little one is. By walking into their room you will also be able to smell if they have done a dirty nappy. I also think it's a lovely time to say one more goodnight to them and make sure they are in a comfortable position.

FACT When feeding your baby a bottle, have you noticed they can drink without stopping? Until approximately seven months old, babies can breathe and swallow at the same time. If they get congested, they are no longer able to do this and can refuse to feed as a result.

Week 30 Day 2

If you are starting to make friends with others who have little ones of a similar age, you will undoubtedly talk about their development and milestones. This is just a reminder that every baby will do things at different speeds, so please don't get concerned or compare if their baby is at a different stage to yours.

'Just like seeds, children grow at different rates
and bloom at different times.'
Author unknown

TIP Keep a baby nail file by your little one's changing table so it's always to hand and you can file their nails when needed. My advice is to do one nail a night, rather than doing all their fingers and toes in one sitting. That way your baby won't get cross and frustrated by having to stay still for a long period of time. This keeps your little one's nails tidy and trim and will prevent them from scratching themselves.

Week 30 Day 3

ACTIVITY Hold your baby on your knee and jig them up and down while you sing 'Humpty Dumpty'. Holding your baby securely and tip them backwards when you sing 'had a great fall' – and repeat if they are enjoying themselves!

Humpty Dumpty sat on a wall
Humpty Dumpty had a great fall
All the king's horses and all the king's men
Couldn't put Humpty together again

TIP If you haven't already, swap your baby's pram seat from the bassinet to the second stage. Your baby will love being able to see out around them while you go for a walk and it will also help them practise their sitting skills.

REMINDER This is your reminder to write a letter to your little one to add to their memory box. This month, include tickets or mementos from places that you've visited.

Week 30 Day 4

If your baby isn't having milk during the night-time now, you can start to reduce and then drop their 11 a.m. milk feed over a period of a week. Offer water at their mealtime instead.

If your little one is still waking at night to feed, don't drop any milk feeds during the day and try to increase the amount of purée they are enjoying. You want your baby to be consuming all the calories they need during the day, so they can sleep well at night without waking for a feed.

ACTIVITY Create your own sensory room for your little one. Create a safe area on the floor and close the curtains to make it dark. Use the following items to provide a variety of sensory experiences:

- Torches
- Christmas tree lights – put the flashing mode on if possible
- Objects with different textures
- Light projector
- Calm music
- Mirrors

Put a few pillows on the floor for you and your little one to relax on and enjoy the surroundings.

Week 30 Day 5

Your baby should ideally be having three to four milk feeds per day.

I find it very hard to overfeed a baby so if your baby is draining bottles, or is hungry soon after a feed, offer them a little bit more at each feed to fill them up for longer. Babies go through growth spurts so you may find some weeks they're hungrier than others. But as a general rule, try to up their milk intake gradually as they grow. Every baby is different, so be guided by them. A baby who is satisfied after their feed will be a happy baby.

ACTIVITY Sing this counting nursery rhyme, using your hands to count down, representing the five frogs.

Five little speckled frogs
Sat on a speckled log,
Eating some most delicious bugs.
Yum yum!
One jumped into the pool
Where it was nice and cool,
Then there were four green speckled frogs.
Glug glug!

Four little speckled frogs (etc.) . . .

Three little speckled frogs (etc.) . . .

Two little speckled frogs (etc.) . . .

One little speckled frog (etc.) . . .

End with: *Then there were NO green speckled frogs. Glug glug!*

Week 30 Day 6

'A mother's hug lasts long after she lets go.'
Author unknown

A lovely way of incorporating a bedtime cuddle is by putting your baby up on your shoulder after their evening milk feed. This is not only a snuggly bonding time, but this will also allow your little one to digest their milk before lying down, setting them up for a comfortable night's sleep.

31 Weeks Old

ACTIVITY Why not try this squat challenge?

1. Stand straight while holding your baby under their arms, roughly 30cm in front of you, keeping your arms bent at the elbow. Take a deep breath in.
2. With a straight back, slowly go down into a squat position so that your hips are parallel with your knees. Breathe out as you lower your body.
3. Slowly come back up again, breathe in and bring your baby close to you for a cuddle.
4. Do five reps today. Aim to do one more rep each day to build up your strength and balance.

TIP When feeding your baby, use bowls and plates that have in-built suction pads. These will stick firmly to your baby's high-chair tray or the table and stop your little one from picking them up and spilling food everywhere.

Week 31 Day 1

Babies love to put toys in their mouths, so keep them clean while their immune system is still developing. Wipe their toys weekly or as needed with warm, soapy water.

Wash bed toys and teddies in the washing machine regularly. If your baby sucks on their toys they can get really smelly! It's important to keep bed toys clean, especially the ones that your little one rubs near their nose or mouth, to stop infections or spots appearing around their mouths.

Bath toys often get mouldy; it can be tough to clean them and sometimes you do have to replace them. However, try this before throwing anything out: mix a litre of water with half a cup of white vinegar. Soak all the toys in the solution for a few hours then scrub the mould off. If they are squeezy toys, squeeze them while they are underwater to get the solution inside them, then squeeze it out. Repeat this until you can't see any more black bits coming out. Rinse the toys off with warm water and allow to dry.

Generally speaking, I would clean baby toys once every few weeks. If someone in the household is unwell, I would do it more often.

TIP Ball-pit balls and most other toys that don't contain batteries can go in the dishwasher on a low heat setting. If they are really stained, you can use cleaning spray and an old toothbrush to get in between all the cracks!

Week 31 Day 2

If you haven't already, start to gradually reduce your little one's morning nap so it doesn't disrupt their longer, and more important, afternoon sleep. Having a shorter nap in the morning allows you to enjoy more activities with them – meaning it's a great time to start a baby class or a weekly meet-up. Reduce your baby's morning nap by gently rousing them with your voice ten minutes earlier than their usual wake-up time.

TIP I want to pass on this brilliant kitchen hack that will save you time and money. If you have vegetables in the fridge that are going off before you get a chance to use them, chop them up and freeze them in a sealed freezer bag. Most vegetables cook really well straight from frozen.

To make your own sofrito, which is the base to so many meals, add any spare uncooked chopped onions, celery and carrot to a dedicated freezer bag, which you can add to at any time. This will save you time when making meals as everything is already chopped for you.

FOOD FOR THOUGHT Offer your little one a healthy snack at around 10.30 a.m. so lunchtime can be moved slightly later to midday. Healthy snack ideas include yoghurt, rice cakes, fruit and vegetables.

ACTIVITY Fruit comes in all shapes and sizes and varies enormously in texture and feel. Put a few different types of fruit in a bowl for your baby to touch and explore.

FOOD FOR THOUGHT If your little one is teething, you can place these Chicken and Apple Balls in a fridge to cool; your baby can enjoy them cold so they are soothing on their gums.

Ingredients

2 chicken breasts, chopped roughly
1 apple, grated and the juice squeezed out
½ small onion, roughly chopped
½ piece of wholemeal bread, broken into small pieces
1 egg
A handful of fresh parsley
4 tablespoons plain flour
Oil for cooking

1. Put the chicken, apple, onion, bread, egg and parsley into a food processor and blitz until everything is combined.
2. Mould the chicken mix into small round shapes, about 3cm in diameter. Then spread the flour onto a plate and roll the balls in flour.
3. Cook the balls in a pan with oil until cooked through in the middle. Keep turning them often so they don't burn on one side. I always cut one open from the batch to make sure it is fully cooked through. You may need to do a couple of batches, depending on the size of your pan.

TIP To mix things up, swap the apple for chopped dried apricots.

Week 31 Day 4

When it comes to learning, no one does it faster than your baby, and the more you repeat things, the easier it is for them to learn and master new skills.

FACT Research has shown that a baby's first words are related to their environment, the words that they consistently hear and what they are exposed to.

Start to focus on key words that are simple for your baby to understand and that will help them in their day-to-day life, such as 'mamma', 'dadda', 'hello' and 'bye bye'. Key words should be functional and meaningful. Functional words are those that your baby can understand and use to meet their needs, for example 'water,' 'more' and 'milk'. Meaningful words are people's names and things like 'tractor', 'ball' and 'plane'.

ACTIVITY Teach your little one how to do a high five by holding your hand up, touching theirs and saying, 'High five!' You will be amazed at how quickly they learn the action to go with the words. A high five is an instant way of communicating with a baby that they are important and deserve your attention. This tactile communication conveys positive emotion and is a form of encouragement.

Week 31 Day 5

ACTIVITY Try playing crinkle toes! If you receive any packaging with crinkly brown paper inside, keep the paper to put under your little one's feet as they kick on their playmat. The paper will feel and sound different to your baby, encouraging them to stretch, kick and explore.

MINDFULNESS Schedule in some downtime for yourself; plan a relaxing bath and treat it like a meeting so that it's non-negotiable and something for you to look forward to.

FOOD FOR THOUGHT Your baby can now enjoy Sunday lunch with the whole family! Either purée the meal or cut the meat up so it's easier to chew, slicing the vegetables into easy-to-hold finger food. I find Yorkshire puddings are always a huge hit as a finger food!

Week 31 Day 6

FACT Music can help form social bonds between people.

Do you have a song that is special to you both or reminds you of your little one? This could become 'your song' and a special memory for you both in the future.

'Bringing people together is what music has always done best.'
Rob Sheffield, music journalist

ACTIVITY I find that babies can get overwhelmed if they see a whole array of toys in front of them and they find it hard to focus on one activity. Group toys together and put some away for a few weeks – when you bring them back out it's like having new toys!

TIP If your little one is having formula, keep the plastic scoops. Wash and dry them and keep them in a freezer bag, as your baby will love playing with them in water or sand when they are older.

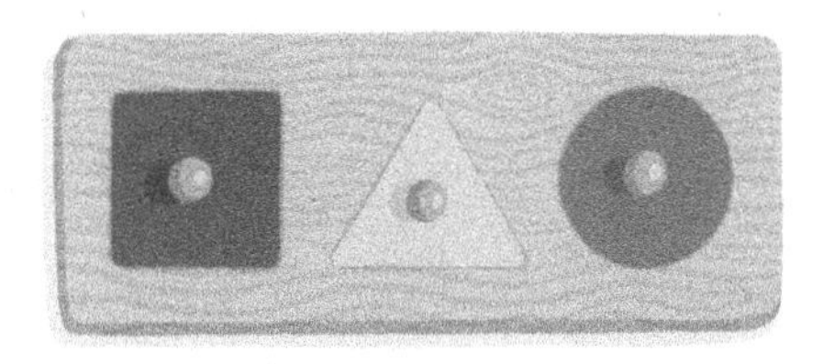

32 Weeks Old

Cheese, cheese, cheese!

FACT Cheese is part of a healthy diet for your little one as it contains calcium, vitamins and protein.

Adding a cheese sauce to your baby's purée will often encourage them to eat a bit more, as they enjoy the creamy consistency.

ACTIVITY Make a batch of Cheese Sauce and freeze in cubes, then pop them into freezer bags.

1. Melt a knob of butter in a pan over a low heat, then stir in an equal quantity of flour to make a roux. Whisk in a little milk, then slowly add more milk to make a white sauce, stirring continuously to stop any lumps appearing.
2. Continue to stir over the heat until the sauce thickens, then add grated Cheddar cheese.

TIP The cheese sauce can be the base for so many different, tasty meals for your baby. You can add it to any protein, with potato and vegetables, and you have a wholesome meal. Try these recipe ideas:

- Tuna pasta bake
- Broccoli and cauliflower cheese
- Lasagne
- Macaroni cheese

FOOD FOR THOUGHT Grated cheese is also a good finger food for your little one to practise their fine motor skills as they learn to pick up the small pieces.

Week 32 Day 1

FACT Your baby's left and right brain coordination will be improved by crawling. This is because they are practising sight, movement and hearing all at the same time.

Crawling will be the first bit of independence for your baby – it's a big milestone! Babies all crawl at different ages, most commonly between seven and ten months old.

You can encourage your baby to crawl by continuing to practise lots of tummy time so they get used to the feeling of being on their fronts and build up their body strength.

The first signs of crawling are often when they start rocking backwards and forwards, sometimes sliding backwards and then pulling themselves forward with their arms, with their tummies still on the floor, like an army crawl. Once they learn to get their legs underneath and push off, they'll be away!

Some babies miss the crawling stage altogether and learn to do the 'bum shuffle' instead. It's amazing how fast they can go bouncing along on their bottoms! This is absolutely fine and no need to worry. They will stick with whichever technique they find the fastest.

ACTIVITY You can help your baby gain the forward motion by placing your hands behind your baby's feet, so they can push against them.

TIP I advise fitting stair gates at the top and bottom of the stairs as soon as your baby can move independently. This will stop any tumbles, or your baby disappearing up the stairs without you.

Week 32 Day 2

FACT A bowl of porridge for breakfast provides your body with more fibre than a slice of wholemeal toast, so it's a great choice for both you and your little one.

Babies and toddlers under the age of two years old should only be given whole milk as opposed to semi-skimmed or skimmed. This is due to the higher calcium levels they need for their bones and teeth.

FOOD FOR THOUGHT Try starting your and your baby's day with some porridge, made using whole milk. Once the oats have nearly cooked through you can add some of the following:

- Chia seeds – full of fibre and omega-3
- Flax seeds – full of fibre and omega-3
- Cinnamon – anti-inflammatory properties
- Blueberries – frozen blueberries turn the porridge purple and are packed with antioxidants!

TIP Crack an egg into the porridge when it's still on the hob and mix it through the oats while cooking. It sounds very strange but I've tried it and I promise your baby will never know. It actually makes the porridge creamier! It provides protein, iron and choline – which helps the brain and nervous system regulate memory, mood and muscle control.

Week 32 Day 3

Blowing bubbles is a fun and safe sensory experience that your baby will love.

Put some music on, talk to them using expressive words such as 'wow!', 'up, up, up' and 'ooooh!' to encourage them to watch or follow the bubbles and then 'pop' them with their finger.

Blowing bubbles is great for encouraging your baby to crawl as they will want to follow the floating bubbles.

ACTIVITY Make your own bubble mix; all you need is washing-up liquid and water.

1. Pour 50ml of washing-up liquid into a container.
2. Slowly add in 300ml of water.
3. Mix gently with a spoon and let the mixture rest.

If you don't have a bubble wand you can use a fly swatter instead!

Sing this song while blowing the bubbles:

Bubbles, bubbles everywhere
Bubbles, bubbles, bubbles in the air
Bubbles, bubbles floating down
Bubbles, bubbles hit the ground. POP!

TIP Add a teaspoon of sugar to your mixture and leave to rest overnight to improve the quality of your bubbles and make them last longer.

MINDFULNESS

'Today I placed a bubble of happiness around myself
and nothing negative can get in.'
Gaia Blooming

Week 32 Day 4

FOOD FOR THOUGHT Batch-make these Fish Cakes for you and your baby to enjoy. They freeze well and make a great finger food.

Ingredients
300g potatoes, peeled and cut into small cubes
200g salmon fillet
1 lemon
50g butter
dash of milk
3 spring onions, finely sliced
a handful of flat-leaf parsley, chopped
4 tablespoons plain flour, plus additional for dusting
2 eggs, beaten
100g breadcrumbs

1. Preheat the oven to 180°C.
2. Cook the potatoes in boiling water until soft.
3. Meanwhile, wrap the salmon fillets in tin foil with a slice of lemon on each fillet, place on a baking tray and bake in the oven for 12 minutes. Retain any unused lemon.
4. Drain and mash the potatoes while they are still piping hot with a knob of butter and a splash of milk, and leave to cool down.
5. Flake the cooked salmon into the bowl, adding the spring onions, chopped parsley, flour, 1 beaten egg and a pinch of salt and pepper (optional). Grate over the zest of the remaining lemon, then mash everything together.
6. Divide the mixture into 8 patties, about 2cm thick. Make mini portions for your baby.
7. Coat the fishcakes in flour, dip in a plate of the remaining beaten egg and cover in breadcrumbs. Cool in the fridge.
8. Heat some oil in a frying pan over a medium heat, add the fishcakes and cook for about 4 minutes on each side, or until golden and cooked through. Your baby's smaller fish cakes will take less time to cook.

Week 32 Day 5

FACT Some babies will miss the crawling stage altogether and go straight to cruising and walking.

TIP Lay a variety of textures out on the floor for your little one to explore as a sensory experience. Bubble wrap, wrapping paper and foam packaging all make enticing sounds that will encourage your baby to move towards them.

MINDFULNESS Start the day the right way: be grateful for everything you have, and make a habit of thinking of one grateful thought when you wake. Something as simple as consciously smiling at yourself in the mirror can create a positive start to your day.

'Mindfulness isn't difficult. We just need to remember to do it.'
Sharon Salzberg, meditation teacher and author

Week 32 Day 6

When your baby coos and chats, respond in a tone of voice that makes them think that what they just said is the most exciting thing. Expressions like 'wow!' and 'really?' will engage their attention and make them want to continue the conversation.

ACTIVITY Pretend to sneeze and see if your baby likes the sound 'achoo!' and the action of your head nodding at the same time. For some reason, this seems to be something that babies find amusing. Other sounds your baby might enjoy are 'wowie!' and 'uh oh!'

TIP Minced meat is far easier for your little one to chew and digest at the moment. You can make meatballs with a variety of different meat including chicken, turkey, pork, beef and lamb. Meatballs on their own are a great finger food, or they can be part of a bigger meal with a sauce, carbohydrate and vegetable.

33 Weeks Old

ACTIVITY Put some sprigs of herbs on a baking tray and let your little one explore their senses by touching, smelling and tasting the herbs. Stay with your baby at all times when doing this activity to make sure that licking the herbs doesn't turn into your little one eating them!

FOOD FOR THOUGHT Instead of buying sweetened yoghurts in the supermarket that can often have additives in them, mix natural yoghurt with homemade fruit purées.

MINDFULNESS Text a friend you haven't spoken to in a while.

Week 33 Day 1

Learning the art of imitation is an important foundation skill for your little one when it comes to their communication.

FACT Copying your baby's actions and the sounds they make will trigger their 'mirror neurons'. These are nerve cells that are activated when your baby watches you do or say something, understands it and then tries to imitate.

Once they have learnt to copy you, they will start to make their own sounds and gestures without you having to prompt them. They may even start doing it because they want you to copy them. This is also a great opportunity to teach them how to take turns, which will help with their conversational skills later on.

ACTIVITY Encourage your baby to copy you by doing the following: blowing raspberries, coughing, waving, clapping and making animal sounds.

Week 33 Day 2

ACTIVITY To help your baby learn to crawl, place them on a comfortable mat with some enticing toys just out of their reach. Encourage movement by shaking the toys and using funny voices that tempt your little one to try and move towards them.

TIP It's really hard for girls to crawl in dresses as their legs get caught in the material, so it's best to dress them in rompers or comfortable leggings. If you have lots of hard floors in your house, you might want to dress them in soft, thick trousers to prevent sore knees. You can also buy knee pads if your little one crawls on stone floors or you see their knees starting to get red and sore. Moisturise their legs every evening to help them recover during the night.

FOOD FOR THOUGHT This Ice Lolly Breakfast makes a fun change for your baby. To make, simply blend the fruit, or fruits, of your choice with some natural yoghurt, and pour them into lolly moulds to freeze. You could try mango, raspberry, strawberry and banana. I would always offer something more substantial, like a piece of toast or some porridge, to go alongside the lollies, as they won't fill hungry tummies for long.

Week 33 Day 3

Five reasons why singing nursery rhymes is good for your baby:

- It helps their speech and language development.
- It releases feel-good endorphins.
- It keeps them engaged.
- It's good for bonding with you.
- It calms them down if they're going through a fretful moment!

ACTIVITY Sing 'Incy Wincy Spider' to your little one while they are in the bath tonight. Use the actions and see if they will copy you.

Incy Wincy Spider climbed up the water spout
Down came the rain and washed poor Incy out
Out came the sunshine and dried up all the rain
And Incy Wincy Spider climbed up the spout again

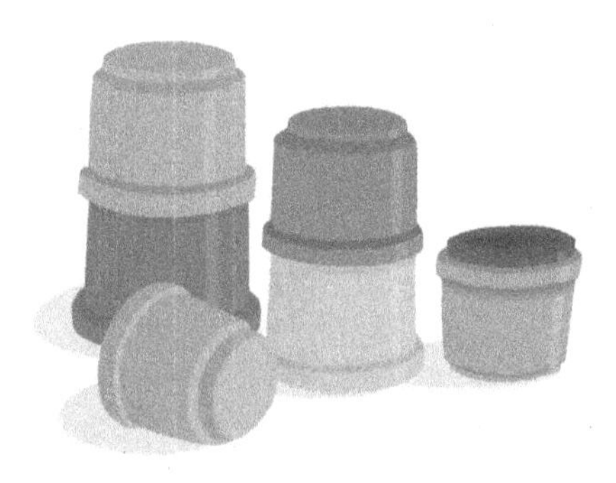

Week 33 Day 4

When you are tired and sleep-deprived, the first person you will take it out on is your nearest and dearest . . . Remember that!

TIP Help your relationship by asking about your partner's day and respect you have both had it tough in different ways. One person is usually at home with the children while the other might be out at work. Understand both points of view and acknowledge that you've both had long days. A small gesture such as cooking a nice dinner can go a long way.

Praise each other: parenting is a full-time and relentless job.

MINDFULNESS When you're feeling pulled in all directions, take a few deep breaths and locate the still centre of yourself.

'Within you, there is a stillness and a sanctuary to which you can retreat at any time and be yourself.'
Hermann Hesse, poet and novelist

Week 33 Day 5

You never know when you may get delayed, break down or get stuck in a traffic jam on a road journey. You will be extremely thankful to have some extra essentials with you to make sure your little one is happy and has everything they need.

ACTIVITY Make an emergency car kit to keep in your boot. Include:

- Nappies
- Wipes
- A spare change of clothes
- Bottle of water
- Ready-made formula (if your baby is formula fed)
- Blanket

TIP Plan journeys around nap times. I always try to leave on a long journey just before babies and toddlers are due to have their afternoon nap. Don't leave in rush-hour traffic – it's better to wait. Babies especially love the motion of the car, so it's better to leave when you can hopefully keep moving. Sometimes having tea and bathtime, getting in PJs and then leaving at bedtime is a good way to have a quiet journey, as your little one will just sleep and can be lifted into bed when you reach your destination.

Week 33 Day 6

Once your baby starts crawling, be even more cautious if you have a dog. Even the most placid dog can sometimes become snappy with babies who are now a threat to their toys. Never leave your baby on their own with a dog or cat. Babies will pull tails and scratch without realising and animals will naturally react.

Keep your eye on your little one at all times at this age; they will be off at huge speeds and can disappear into another room in the blink of an eye! Your baby has no common sense at this age, so they will grab anything, tug at tablecloths, open drawers and empty cupboards. Remove anything breakable within their reach and from the beginning tell your baby 'Na na na' to anything you don't want them to touch or open. Distract them and be consistent when telling them something's not for them, which will help them learn not to touch certain things.

TIP If you have a dog or an area that can't be baby-proofed, you may want to purchase a safe space like a playpen to pop your baby in when you go to the loo or need to concentrate on something else for a few minutes. You can set up a travel cot instead of buying a wooden playpen. Being in a playpen means your baby will be safe from harm. Place a comfortable pillow and some age-appropriate books and toys in there so it's a fun place, not somewhere they feel they are being abandoned!

34 Weeks Old

Babies start suffering from separation anxiety any time from six months on, but it often peaks between eight months and a year old. When you leave your child, whether it's to go to the shops for half an hour or elsewhere for a week, always say goodbye and tell them how long it will be until you come back. Do this from when they are small babies.

Even if they get upset or clingy, it's much better that they know you've gone and that you left deliberately – it makes them feel much more secure and they know that nothing bad has happened to you.

I know from looking after lots of little ones when their parents leave that children who have said goodbye settle a lot quicker and are much happier in the long run. Sometimes parents feel it's best to slip out while their child is playing happily, but I find that a child who is left without saying goodbye often becomes more clingy to their parents. They never leave their side in case their parents sneak out when they're in the other room. A child who grows up knowing that their carer won't go without telling them first is happy to play and go off independently.

REMINDER Here is a reminder to take your monthly photo today of your baby alongside your chosen teddy bear. This is number eight of your twelve photographs, which you can keep to document your little one's growth during their first year.

Week 34 Day 1

FACT Big developmental changes, such as crawling and walking, may disturb your baby's sleep for a few nights, due to their brain and body finding it hard to relax after mastering such an exciting milestone.

If your baby does wake, go into their room quietly, give them a cuddle and remind them it's bedtime. Use their usual sleep cues to put them back to bed. This should only last for a few nights.

ACTIVITY Make a homemade obstacle course with cushions for your baby to climb over. This will build their strength and enhance their problem-solving skills.

TIP Have a stair gate at the bottom and at the top of your stairs to prevent your crawling baby or toddler falling down them. There are lots of different types available to suit the size and shape of your staircase.

Week 34 Day 2

ACTIVITY Give your baby a lemon to hold and explore. The smell and texture will be fascinating to them! See if you notice them passing the lemon from one hand to the other.

FACT Between seven and eight months of age your baby will begin to pass toys from one hand to the other and bang them together to make a noise, meaning their movements will become more and more coordinated.

FOOD FOR THOUGHT Try rice cakes with nut butter on top for your little one's snack today.

Week 34 Day 3

Make this rhyme part of your little one's bedtime routine. Sing the song and do the actions with them as a fun activity before they go to bed:

Teddy bear, teddy bear, turn around
Teddy bear, teddy bear, touch the ground
Teddy bear, teddy bear, climb the stairs
Teddy bear, teddy bear, say your prayers
Teddy bear, teddy bear, turn out the light
Teddy bear, teddy bear, say 'good night'.

ACTIVITY Spend some time today cleansing your little one's highchair thoroughly with warm, soapy water. You probably give it a wipe down after every meal, but it's surprising how much grime builds up in those hard-to-reach places and underneath the tray over time. Get into all the cracks by using a toothbrush for awkward areas. Lastly, I like to take the highchair outside and hose it down, leaving it in the sunshine to dry off.

Week 34 Day 4

Today is all about safety.

It is time to start baby-proofing your house while your little one is close to learning to crawl! I recommend you take the following precautions in your home when you have a soon-to-be crawling baby, even if you don't intend to leave them unsupervised.

Accidents can happen very easily in a matter of seconds, so it is important to do what you can to help prevent them happening.

- When loading the dishwasher, make sure all knives and forks are pointing downwards so there are no sharp edges for little hands!
- When you are using the hob for cooking, make sure pans are placed towards the back with handles also pointing backwards, keeping them out of easy reach.
- Drawers and cupboards that contain sharp objects must have child safety locks on them. This also applies to those containing any cleaning supplies such as dishwasher tablets, laundry liquid and bleach.
- Never leave a grill or oven door open when children are around.
- Make sure kettles are placed towards the back of the worktop so that children can't pull them down and burn themselves.
- Keep medication out of reach or, even better, in a lockable cabinet.
- Use a non-slip mat in the bath.
- Empty the bath after the children get out in case they fall in.

Week 34 Day 5

Babies this age often start protesting, rolling over or wriggling away when you lie them down to change their nappy.

TIP Keep a small toy by the changing mat which they can hold and play with. Something like a little baby toothbrush or toy animal is enough to distract them while you change their nappy and hold their attention by chatting and singing to them. When they try to twist and turn over, gently hold them so they can't roll. Say, 'Na na na, we always lie still for one minute while we change you.' If you are consistent, they quickly learn they have to lie still while their nappy is being changed and they stop fighting it, otherwise it becomes a long and messy process!

FACT Babies have flat feet for the first few years. The arch in their feet starts to develop around their second birthday.

Week 34 Day 6

FACT Babies at this age become sensitive to your tone of voice and start to understand what you are saying by the way you say it and by your facial expressions to match.

Research has shown that 'parentese' – communicating with your baby using a 'sing-song' voice and varying the tone – makes it easier for them to understand the message even before they understand the meaning of the words.

Think about the tone of your voice when your baby does something pleasing. Your response with a happy and excited tone of voice will make them want to do it again.

ACTIVITY Sing this popular nursery rhyme with your little one today while doing the actions. If you have a toy bus then bring the song to life even more by showing your baby the bus as you sing.

The wheels on the bus go round and round,
round and round, round and round
The wheels on the bus go round and round
All through the town.

The wipers on the bus go swish swish swish,
swish swish swish, swish swish swish
The wipers on the bus go swish, swish, swish
All through the town.

(etc.) . . .

35 Weeks Old

Your baby may experience distress and clinginess at this age if you put them down to get on with other chores.

My advice for making your baby feel as secure as possible is to give them your time when you have it available. Spend time on the floor playing with them, communicating and being tactile so they're not having to call out for your attention.

When you need to get on with things in the house, give your baby something to play with – a wooden spoon and saucepan, a treasure basket – or put them on a playmat with some fun things to look at and explore. Continue to talk to your baby so they can hear your voice and know you're not far away. Use distractions they enjoy, such as music.

Clinginess will always increase if your baby is unwell, tired or stressed. It's important not to get cross with them. The more you show your frustration at not being able to put them down, the more upset they will get.

Week 35 Day 1

FACT The cerebellum is an important part of your baby's brain that controls movement and balance. Swinging stimulates the cerebellum, developing your baby's balance and establishing their ability to regulate their emotions.

But, most importantly, being on a swing is fun and exciting! And as we know, feeling happy and laughing is what's best for your little one's mental and physical health.

ACTIVITY A baby swing is the first piece of equipment your little one can enjoy at a playground. Some babies absolutely love the swinging motion and others don't, so make sure you take it nice and slow to begin with!

TIP Use a towel or a cushion to support your baby if they are a little small in the swing. The more supported they feel, the more they will enjoy the experience.

Week 35 Day 2

You can now start to add a few lumps and texture to your baby's meals. Introduce these lumps very slowly so your little one doesn't notice much of a change in consistency.

TIP I would still mix the purées together – for example, mix the potato and mince from a shepherd's pie with some vegetables. I also recommend buying a packet of baby pasta. These pasta pieces are small and easy for your baby to digest, and adding a sauce to them makes a simple meal.

You can offer them a little pudding after lunch and tea if they are still hungry, such as chopped fruit, yoghurt or a fruit purée. Your baby can also start to enjoy breakfast cereals.

REMINDER This is your reminder to write a letter to your little one to add to their memory box. This month, add a coin from the year they were born.

Week 35 Day 3

FACT Your baby's eyesight is now as clear and focused as an adult's . . . isn't that amazing?

ACTIVITY Babies love taking things apart and putting them back together. Fill a little handbag with a few different items such as a toy, a book, a piece of fruit, a sponge and a spoon and let them zip and unzip the items back inside.

FOOD FOR THOUGHT The recommended portion size for starchy food for your little one until they are twelve months old is approximately the size of one slice of bread with crusts, or two slices of bread without the crusts on. Starchy foods include potatoes, rice, pasta and cereals.

Week 35 Day 4

Setting boundaries, saying 'no' and disciplining your little one – in the right way – is such an important part of growing up. Discipline should never involve physical punishment.

It sounds strange talking about 'disciplining' a baby, but babies understand the concept of 'no' from as young as eight months old – and this is important so they know to look to us for guidance on what is dangerous and safe.

TIP Instead of saying 'no' to your baby, say – in a talking and never shouting tone – 'Na na na, don't do that because . . .' Tone is so vital when communicating with your baby.

As soon as your little one is on the move, you will need to start guiding them on what they can and can't do, or where they can and can't go. This is for their own safety, and it's their first experience of rules and 'discipline'.

Always talk to your baby, even from this early age, and explain why you're saying 'na na na'. If they get upset, distract them by looking out a window, pointing out something in the room or showing them some toys. Be confident that you are doing the right thing; don't feel guilty if they protest!

For example, if they are pulling your hair, you can say, 'Na na na, that hurts, don't pull my hair please,' and offer them a toy instead to distract.

It's amazing how quickly they learn!

Week 35 Day 5

ACTIVITY Babies love the feeling and sound of running water . . . try a sink bath today with your little one. Let your baby sit and play in the running water and then give them some toys to fill with water and pour from.

FOOD FOR THOUGHT Try these easy and nutritious Cheese and Spinach Muffins – you can make a whole batch and freeze them for a quick snack for you or your baby. You can also add all sorts of other savoury ingredients to these muffins: sweetcorn, ham, grated carrot, red pepper, spring onion . . . whatever takes your fancy!

Ingredients
1 egg
175ml milk
50ml olive oil
225g self-raising flour
75g Cheddar cheese, grated
50g mozzarella, cubed
A handful of spinach leaves, washed and chopped
Butter or oil to grease the muffin tray

1. Preheat the oven to 180°C and grease 10 muffin tin moulds with butter or oil.
2. Mix the egg, milk and oil together in a bowl.
3. Combine the rest of the ingredients and divide the mixture equally between the 10 muffin tin moulds.
4. Bake in the oven for 20 minutes, until cooked through and golden brown.

Week 35 Day 6

FACT Burns are most likely to happen at home from a baby knocking over a cup of hot tea, getting splashed by a hot liquid that's being carried by an adult, grabbing tablecloths and pulling the contents over them and by being put in a bath that's too hot.

TIP I hope your little one never gets a burn, but here's a step-by-step guide if they do:

1. Cool the burn using cool running water for at least 20 minutes.
2. Keep the rest of the child's body warm with a blanket.
3. Cover the cooled burn with a dressing that won't stick. Cling film is ideal: it will help with pain relief and prevent infection.
4. Always seek medical advice.

HOW TO Follow the link on this QR code to watch my video on what to do if your baby suffers a burn.

36 Weeks Old

It's great to be able to take your little one out to restaurants and enjoy a family meal with them.

You can order food off a menu for them when you are eating out. It's good for them to try different foods. Don't think you have to order off the children's menu, though; they can share what you order, or I often find a starter is a great size for a baby – a fish cake or bowl of soup, for example, is perfect.

I would rather they enjoy something like risotto, a pasta dish, fish pie, lasagne or a mild curry and rice, than chicken nuggets and chips. All you have to do is mash the food so it's the right texture for your baby.

Stay away from really salty foods and if you're unsure what's in the dish, ask the waiting staff. If you order chips or vegetables, ask for them without added salt – but don't panic if there is some salt in their meal, as a little bit of salt won't harm them on a one-off occasion.

Most restaurants will have a highchair, but if they don't, sit them in their pram by the table.

TIP To stop any breakages, remove any glasses and cutlery that are within your baby's reach when you sit down!

Week 36 Day 1

FOOD FOR THOUGHT Butter is made from saturated fat, whereas margarine is made from healthy fats. Use margarine as the healthier option for both you and your little one. Olive oil-based margarines are the best choice.

ACTIVITY Add ball-pit balls to your baby's bath to create some bathtime fun! This activity will encourage their sensory development, creativity, imagination and gross motor skills.

TIP If your baby has suddenly started waking early every morning with a dirty nappy, try this trick: dilute prune juice with cooled boiled water and offer them sips throughout the day. This should change their cycle and ensure they do a poo before they go to bed. After a few days, the early waking should stop.

Week 36 Day 2

Have you noticed your little one getting excited and banging objects together in their hands? For them, this isn't just about making a noise, it's an experiment to see what happens.

This is called cause and effect and is a part of their development. Playing this way helps your baby learn that their actions are causing something to happen.

ACTIVITY Exposing your little one to musical instruments will help to enhance their gross and fine motor skills, and speech and language development. Try getting your baby to copy you with a rhythmic beat, shake an instrument or bang on some drums.

TIP You can purchase TV straps to stop flat-screen televisions from tipping if you have them on a stand instead of mounted on the wall.

FACT Fruit juice is not suitable for your baby due to its sugar content, even when diluted, as it can lead to tooth decay. Due to the sweet taste, your little one is also likely to drink more than usual, which then fills them up and causes them not to eat as well at mealtimes.

FOOD FOR THOUGHT These Cauliflower and Cheese Bites are another healthy snack for both you and your baby. They can be frozen for up to three months. To defrost, ensure they are piping hot then leave to cool before serving.

Ingredients
1 cauliflower head
100g Cheddar cheese, grated
Half a small courgette, grated
1 egg
3 tablespoons plain flour

1. Preheat the oven to 180°C.
2. Cut the cauliflower into pieces and simmer in a pan of water for 10 minutes, then drain completely.
3. Blitz the cauliflower in a blender until it resembles grains of rice.
4. Mix the cauliflower with the cheese, courgette, egg and flour.
5. Place tablespoon-size amounts of the mix onto a baking tray lined with baking paper and pop in the oven for 10 minutes. Turn the bites over and then cook for another 10 minutes. Serve warm or cold.

Week 36 Day 4

Loose, comfortable clothing is perfect for your soon-to-be crawler. Leggings without buttons are easier to move around in than jeans. The more freedom of movement they have, the more they will want to practise their crawling skills.

TIP Look around your home and if you have any sharp corners at your little one's height, for example a coffee table, use corner protectors in case your baby falls on them.

ACTIVITY Treat yourself to a foot scrub this evening when your little one is in bed.

1. Pour five cups of warm water and one cup of milk into a large tub.
2. In a separate bowl, mix baby oil and sugar together to make a thick paste.
3. Soak your feet in the tub for ten minutes.
4. Massage the paste into your feet while they are still slightly damp and allow to penetrate for a further five minutes before rinsing off.

Week 36 Day 5

TIP If you feel daily chores are getting on top of you and you'd like to be more organised, try to block out thirty minutes per day while your baby naps. This gives you the time to pay bills, make calls and keep on top of other general admin and will instantly help you feel more organised and on top of things.

FOOD FOR THOUGHT These Tuna and Sweetcorn Fritters make a tasty finger food for your baby. They can be kept in the fridge for 3–4 days or frozen individually on a baking sheet so they don't stick together.

Ingredients
1 can tuna, drained
½ tin sweetcorn
1 egg
A handful of grated Cheddar or mozzarella cheese
2 tablespoons plain flour

1. Mix all the ingredients together in a bowl.
2. In a large pan, heat a teaspoon of oil then add the tuna mix in tablespoon-size amounts. Cook the fritters for 2 minutes and then use a spatula to turn over and cook for a further 2 minutes, until golden brown.
3. Serve hot or cold.

Week 36 Day 6

As your baby grows, you will need to keep adjusting your home to their changing size and abilities. You need to always keep thinking one step ahead so you can keep your little one safe.

ACTIVITY Walk through your home and if you have any blind cords by windows that are hanging loosely, tie them up high immediately and fix them to the wall as soon as possible so that they are out of reach for your little one and don't pose a strangulation risk.

TIP When sitting in their highchair, your baby's hips, knees and feet should all be at a ninety-degree angle. By having a footrest, your little one will be more comfortable and less likely to fidget.

37 Weeks Old

Fresh air is beneficial for everyone and it's good to remove the walls sometimes. If it's a dry day today, create an outdoor play-room in the garden or at the park. Put down a blanket and scatter around some toys for your little one to enjoy under the canopy of the sky, rather than being confined to a room.

ACTIVITY Enjoy a picnic together. This could be in your garden or while out on a walk. It's fun to come away from the highchair and table sometimes and deviate from the norm.

FOOD FOR THOUGHT Here are some picnic food ideas:

- Quiche
- Rice cakes with nut butter
- Meatballs
- Falafel
- Cooked vegetables
- Mini sandwiches
- Frittata
- Egg muffins
- Chopped fruit
- Pesto pasta

Week 37 Day 1

Your eight-month-old is very curious, but also has a very short attention span!

You might find your baby moves on from one toy or game to the next in a matter of minutes. Or you might find one toy really captures their attention and fascinates them. This will be a different toy for each baby.

Toys don't need to be expensive or electronic; babies also love simple playthings such as musical instruments and wooden puzzles.

Sometimes the simplest toys get the most use, like building blocks or a cardboard box.

This is because they provide un-ending play . . . your baby can make them what they want them to be and the play develops and grows with their imagination.

The more a toy 'does', the less your baby has to do. So for some toys, once they've pressed the flashing light or heard the music, that's the end of the play.

ACTIVITY Save some cardboard boxes that would usually go in the recycling bin and let your little one pull the lids on and off. You could hide an object inside the box for your baby to find.

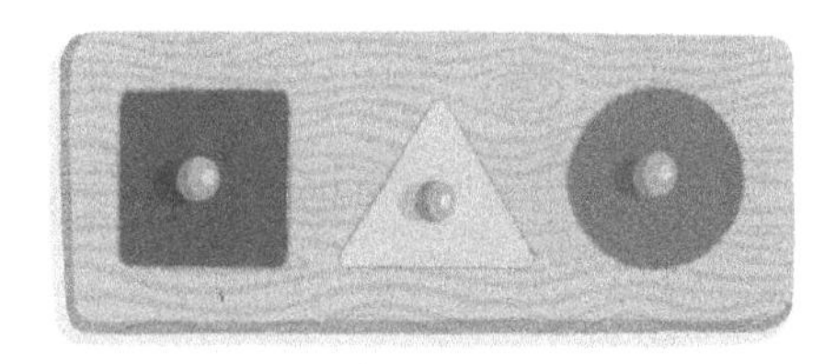

Week 37 Day 2

FACT Quinoa contains essential amino acids that the body needs, yet can't make on its own. Amino acids are crucial to your baby's growth and development: they build muscle, repair body tissue, break down food, provide energy and boost their immune system.

FOOD FOR THOUGHT These Sweet Potato and Quinoa Bites are delicious served warm or cold with natural yoghurt or hummus.

Ingredients
1 sweet potato, peeled and boiled until soft
200g quinoa, cooked according to packet instructions
100g Cheddar cheese, grated
1 carrot, peeled and grated

1. Preheat the oven to 180°C.
2. In a bowl, combine all the ingredients. Use a teaspoon to make little patties, and place them on a baking tray lined with baking paper.
3. Cook in the oven for 15 minutes, then turn them over and cook for a further 15 minutes until crispy on the outside and slightly golden brown.

TIP This is another reminder to check your baby's car seat straps sit parallel to their shoulders when fastened. You may need to alter them as your little one is growing.

Week 37 Day 3

Everything can be fixed. If you don't like the way something is . . . it can change. For example, if your little one isn't sleeping or eating well, don't feel overwhelmed, it can be fixed.

Parenting shouldn't feel chaotic or that you are not in control. If it does, please ask for help. Think about what you are finding hard and what you need to change to make things easier.

TIP Ask your partner if they can take your baby out for the morning so you can practise some self-care and reset. Do the same for them in return. Plan something that makes you feel good, such as going for a run or getting your nails done.

FOOD FOR THOUGHT Beware of food containing added sugar. These may be labelled as sucrose, fructose, dextrose or glucose syrup. Little ones under two years old don't need any added sugar in their diet.

Week 37 Day 4

MINDFULNESS You will often hear children exclaim 'wow!' at something, but how often do *you* soak in the amazement and wonder of the world around you? Take the time to stop and look and reflect on something you see. It could be the size of a huge building or the light coming through the trees. Take some deep breaths, think about how it was created and smile at the wonder of its being.

FACT The healthiest cooking oils are olive oil and rapeseed oil. They are both high in monounsaturated fatty acids, which are good for heart health. Fats and oils provide energy for your baby and, despite their reputation for causing weight gain in adults, they are healthy for babies.

Week 37 Day 5

ACTIVITY Find an empty tissue box and place short pieces of ribbon inside. Show your little one how to pull them out of the top. This is a great activity to further develop your baby's understanding of object permanence.

TIP Babies are known for putting anything and everything in their mouths, so always scan the floor before you let them explore.

MINDFULNESS Set your alarm half an hour before your baby usually wakes in the morning so you can enjoy a peaceful shower without interruptions. While in the shower, focus on the feeling of the water on your skin and what the temperature feels like; how do you actually know if it's hot or cold, what does that feel like? Before using a shower gel or face wash, smell the product.

Week 37 Day 6

FACT When your baby was born, they didn't have fully formed bones, instead they had cartilage, which is softer. Your baby's bones start forming and fusing together as they get older.

ACTIVITY If you have a laundry basket with holes in it, fill it with blankets so it's weighted and poke different materials through the holes from the inside out to make a treasure wall that your baby can reach, feel and pull. You can hook hanging toys on the edge of the basket, poke the hands of soft toys through the holes and even tie brightly coloured ribbons to the basket.

38 Weeks Old

FACT Your baby is learning how to make different sounds with their voice – this is called babbling.

When your baby is babbling, they are practising moving their tongue and lips to copy the sounds they hear. This is why you should encourage babbling by repeating the sounds your little one makes and telling them how clever they are.

After cooing, you will start to hear your baby making consonant sounds such as *da*, *ma* and *ba*.

ACTIVITY Sit with your baby in front of a mirror so they can see your facial expressions and see if they will copy the exaggerated movements of your mouth as you talk to them.

Week 38 Day 1

Independent play is when your baby can happily play on their own.

Encouraging your little one to play by themselves is as important as learning to play in a group, as it allows them to be confident, improve their focus and be content in their own company and thoughts.

Allow short periods of time throughout your day where you are supervising your baby playing, but you are not interacting with them.

FOOD FOR THOUGHT Mackerel is full of omega-3 fatty acids and is also a good source of vitamin D. However, it is also high in mercury so should only be eaten once or twice a week. Try it on toast with this easy recipe:

Ingredients

2 smoked mackerel fillets (tinned is fine), skinned
2 tablespoons cream cheese
Flesh of 1 avocado
Juice from half a lemon
1 spring onion

1. Blend everything together until smooth and creamy – it's as simple as that!
2. Serve on toast or bread.

Week 38 Day 2

Sharing and taking turns is an important part of growing up and a skill that should be encouraged from an early age.

ACTIVITY Sit opposite your little one and get their attention by playing with a toy that is small enough to fit in one hand. Say to them, 'It's (your baby's name) turn,' as you give them the toy. Once they have inspected the toy, hold your hand out and say, 'Please can I have a turn?' Your baby will hopefully find this funny, like a game, and although they won't always give it back to you, they learn to understand what you are asking.

REMINDER Here is a reminder to take your monthly photo today of your baby alongside your chosen teddy bear. This is number nine of your twelve photographs, which you can keep to document your little one's growth during their first year.

Week 38 Day 3

'Every child is an individual with a different growth rate and a varied and vast potential. Respecting the talent that is hidden within each child, we respect their potential to become Kings of their Trade, or Saviors of the World to come.'
Natasa Pantovic Nuit, author of Conscious Parenting

Now that your baby is approaching nine months old, I have put together eight milestones which you can tick off if your little one has accomplished them.

If they haven't reached all of them yet, I'm sure it's nothing to worry about, but it's a good idea to have a chat with your health visitor. Remember, every baby goes at their own pace.

1. Responds to their name
2. Babbles 'da da da'
3. Bears weight when held up
4. Reaches into a treasure basket
5. Enjoys a game of peekaboo
6. Picks up food, hand to mouth
7. Claps hands
8. Sits unaided

FOOD FOR THOUGHT These tasty Chicken and Apple Burgers make a good finger food for your baby. They can be frozen before or after they are cooked. Line a container with baking paper to stop the burgers sticking to the container before freezing, and put a piece of baking paper between the burgers so you can take one burger out for lunch without having to defrost them all.

Ingredients

700g chicken thighs or breast, skinless and deboned
3 apples, grated and the juice squeezed out
1 onion, chopped
2 garlic cloves, crushed
2 eggs
4 tablespoons plain flour
Oil for cooking

1. Put the chicken, apple, onion, garlic and egg into a food processor and blitz until everything is combined.
2. Mould the chicken mix into burger shapes using your hands. Spread the flour onto a plate and coat the burgers on both sides in flour.
3. If you have time, chill the burgers in the fridge for half an hour, and then fry them in a pan with some oil until completely cooked through in the middle.

Week 38 Day 5

ACTIVITY Sing this popular nursery rhyme with your baby today. Sit them on your knees, facing you, and hold their hands, rowing them back and forth.

The movement of rowing backwards and forwards is a gross motor skill for your little one to master.

Row, row, row your boat
Gently down the stream
Merrily, merrily, merrily, merrily
Life is but a dream

FOOD FOR THOUGHT The beauty of a frittata is that you can add pretty much whatever you have in the fridge! Things you can add to a frittata include leftover veg, cooked meats, cooked potato or cheese. The base of a frittata is whisked egg, and a small amount of plain flour to help it set.

1. Cook any ingredients that need to be softened or cooked, and then layer them in an ovenproof dish.
2. Whisk enough eggs to cover the main ingredients with 1 teaspoon of flour per egg (so if you use 2 eggs, add 2 teaspoons etc).
3. Mix the egg with the main ingredients in the ovenproof dish and pop into the oven at 180°C until the eggs are cooked through and set. The deeper the frittata, the longer it will take to cook.
4. Cut into slices and serve warm, or store in an airtight container in the fridge and serve cold.

TIP Make the frittata quite thin so it's easy for your little one to hold.

Week 38 Day 6

ACTIVITY Thread pipe cleaners through the holes of a colander, using different colours to make it interesting. Let your baby pull them out and try to feed the pipe cleaners back through the holes using their fine motor skills.

This is a great activity for your baby to practise their hand–eye coordination and a good way to keep your little one entertained while you are busy cooking.

39 Weeks Old

ACTIVITY Enjoy some water play with your baby today. Put a towel down on the floor and fill one tray with lukewarm water and the other with cold water. Take their clothes off so they just have their nappy on and let them splash around. Add a few toys to make it more fun while they explore the different temperatures.

MINDFULNESS 'If it won't matter in a year's time, it's not worth worrying about.' I can't remember where I heard this but it's something I recite in my head if something goes wrong or I've made a mistake. It instantly calms my feelings of anxiety or stress.

TIP If your little one's cot is near to a chest of drawers or shelf, make sure they can't reach the contents by putting their hands through the cot bars.

Week 39 Day 1

I encourage mums to breastfeed for as long as they wish to do so. If you are thinking about stopping breastfeeding, it's important to stop feeding gradually. If you stop feeding overnight you will be in a lot of pain and discomfort and run the risk of getting mastitis.

The easiest way to reduce and then stop breastfeeding is to cut the time of each feed by a few minutes each day and replace the milk feed with a bottle.

ACTIVITY Download some podcasts featuring your favourite celebrities to listen to. They can pass the time and help you stay connected to the adult world if you are feeling a little isolated at home with your baby.

Week 39 Day 2

ACTIVITY Spaghetti play is a great sensory activity for babies who like to put everything in their mouths! Picking up and exploring the stringy pasta is great for their fine motor skills, adding to the sensory development aspect of this activity.

1. Cook some spaghetti according to the instructions, though reduce the cooking time by a minute so the pasta doesn't get too soft.
2. Drain the pasta, and run cold water over it to stop the strands sticking together.
3. You can add a little olive oil if it's too dry.

Once the pasta has cooled, let your little one touch it with their hands and feet, show them how to hold it up high and drop it like rain, encourage them to smell the pasta . . . ask them if it's tickly!

TIP Foam door stoppers are a good idea for playrooms and any doors that may slam shut unexpectedly in the wind.

Week 39 Day 3

Talking, labelling and repeating is key for your baby's speech development and something you can incorporate easily into your day – it quickly becomes a habit!

Throughout the day, describe the action you are doing when your baby is paying attention to you. This can be anything from 'Mummy is making a cup of tea now' to 'I'm going to find your ball'. This is called self-talk as you are describing your actions.

Using a phrase such as 'look at you shaking that toy' or 'aren't you clever rolling that ball' is called parallel talk, as you are describing the action your baby is doing.

Try to use both techniques; however, the most important thing is just to focus on talking as much as possible to your little one.

TIP Wrap an elastic band around each page of one of your baby's board books, near the spine of the book. This will open up the book slightly and make it easier for them to turn the pages without getting frustrated.

Week 39 Day 4

Every baby is different. Today, think about your baby's personality.

What makes them excited? What makes them smile or laugh? What scares them, and what makes them cross? What food do they like and what don't they like?

Write all of these down and add it to your little one's memory box.

Note down some ideas of how you can build on these characteristics or encourage a different kind of behaviour. For example, if your baby is scared of water, think about how you can build their confidence.

Week 39 Day 5

ACTIVITY Today try some cornflour play with your little one – all you need is a box (or two) of cornflour and some warm water. Mix some cornflour with a little water in a bowl or tray until it becomes gloopy. Watch how it changes consistency as you handle the mixture. The heat from your hands activates the cornflour and makes it runnier, then it hardens again when not touched. It's my favourite sensory activity to do with babies; you don't have to worry if they put it in their mouths, as it's simply flour. It is also really easy to clean up as it just wipes away with water.

TIP I advise using window locks and make sure you keep the key somewhere safe – do not leave them in the window.

REMINDER This is your reminder to write a letter to your little one to add to their memory box. This month, include a photo of the house they currently live in.

Week 39 Day 6

The saying goes that early readers become life-long readers. Reading is a relaxing activity and a calm bonding time for both of you. It supports your baby's language and speech development, and it is also good for your little one's attention skills as it helps them focus on a story and the pictures on each page.

It's never too early to incorporate gestures while reading a story – the more animated you are, the more your little one will enjoy the experience.

Appropriate story books from this age include 'touch and feel' books, stories that rhyme and those that use repetitive vocabulary.

ACTIVITY Create a cosy and comfortable reading corner for you to enjoy with your baby. Five or six books at floor level are much more enticing to your baby than a whole row of books on a bookshelf. Create a space where you are comfortable so that you want to spend time there. A blanket, bean bag or some big fluffy cushions are all you need.

TIP The best way to read to your baby for their speech and language development is face to face, which gets easier as they get older. By sitting this way, they can watch your expressions and try to copy you, and you can help them point to the pictures, making the book interactive.

40 Weeks Old

ACTIVITY Let your little one play with jelly. The smell, taste and feel of the jelly makes this a great sensory activity for babies who put everything in their mouths! Let them squidge the jelly in their hands and encourage them to taste and smell it.

TIP Do this activity away from their highchair so they don't get confused with tea time!

MINDFULNESS Babies are funny and create even funnier situations . . . at the end of the day, reflect with your partner about amusing scenarios that have taken place. Some of the most stressful moments in life make the best stories!

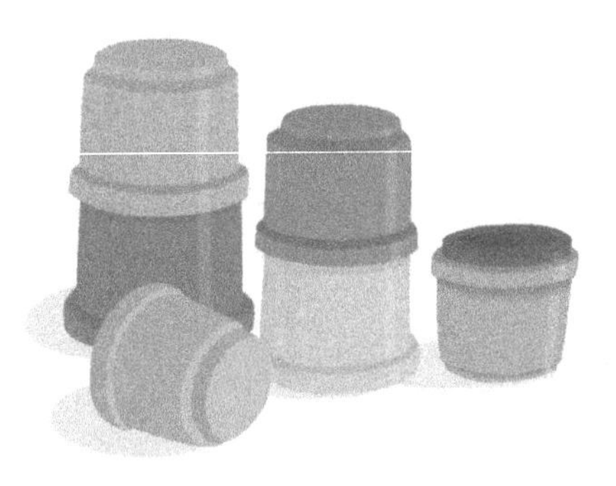

Week 40 Day 1

It's great to have a trusted and familiar face to leave your little one with on the odd evening, allowing yourself some child-free time as parents. It also provides you with another contact to call upon in case of an emergency in addition to family.

I always think a personal recommendation is best when finding a babysitter for your family, so speak to friends and ask if they know anyone good.

Time as a couple, or even on your own, is important when you have a baby so make the most of these services.

TIP Always leave a contact list for your babysitter in case there is an emergency and they can't reach you. This should include your full address in case they need to call for an ambulance. I would also give your babysitter the name and contact number for the restaurant where you are, in case they can't get hold of your mobile phone.

Week 40 Day 2

Babies generally start cruising between nine to twelve months of age. This is their way of trying to walk, while holding onto furniture, toys or your hands for balance. It's important at this stage that your home is safe and any wobbly furniture is secured.

Your baby may walk on their tiptoes for the first six months of cruising. This is fine, but when they stand, encourage them to relax the back of their foot so they put their weight onto the whole of their foot. Babies often stand on tiptoes because their feet are sensitive to the feeling of the floor. Encourage them to stand on lots of different surfaces without shoes or socks on to desensitise their feet!

ACTIVITY Find a push-along toy for your little one to play with. This will encourage your baby to hold onto something and take some steps forward, building both their strength and confidence at the same time.

TIP Remember that your baby can reach higher in their newfound standing position, so be wary of any breakables or hot drinks on coffee tables.

Week 40 Day 3

As a parent, it is amazing to watch your baby develop new skills and grow into a little person. An important developmental milestone around this time is the pincer grip. This is when your baby uses their thumb and forefinger to hold an object. Later in life, this will become useful for everyday activities such as holding a pencil or buttoning up an item of clothing.

It takes lots of practice but they soon master this new skill.

ACTIVITY You can encourage your baby to master their pincer grip by placing small objects or food in front of them, around the size of a pea, and show them how to pick them up. Always do this activity supervised in case of choking.

TIP For your little one to sleep well at night, they need to go to bed with a full tummy. I always serve dinner at 5 p.m. at the earliest, because if they have tea before this it's a long time before their morning feed. If your baby is hungry in the morning, they may start to rise earlier.

Week 40 Day 4

FACT Babies grow at the fastest rate during the first twelve months of life. By the time they turn one year old, the average baby is twice as long as they were when they were born and weigh three times as much.

Your baby may be going through another growth spurt. This could last for a few days so let your baby have a little extra sleep at their nap times if they need it, and go with their increased appetite (see page 33).

ACTIVITY Play 'cereal drop' with your baby. Wash out a milk carton and leave it to dry. Place it next to your little one on the floor and give them a container of cereal. Show them how to pick up a single piece of cereal and drop it into the top of the milk carton. By doing this, they are increasing their concentration and using their fine motor skills pincer grip. When all the cereal is in the milk carton, shake the carton so they hear the fun sound and empty them back in the container to start the game again.

TIP If you have a fireplace, I recommend a fire guard to keep the children away from it.

Week 40 Day 5

At the end of playtime, encourage your baby to watch and help you put the toys away, even if it's just them popping a few cars into a box! This is great practice for the future and tidying up will soon become second nature to them.

TIP Don't take your baby out of their highchair as soon as they are finished, as this becomes a habit and they will always expect to get down as soon as they have lost interest in their food. As your baby gets older and wiser, they will use the phrase 'finished' if they see something they would rather be doing, whereas if they wait a while they are more likely to get a second wind and eat a bit more. You will thank me for this little tip when you are in a restaurant and your little one is happy to sit in their chair while everyone finishes their meal.

MINDFULNESS Your baby will pick up on your stress, so at times when you are feeling frustrated or there's something on your mind, keep this quote in your thoughts.

> 'If you can't do anything about it, then let it go.
> Don't be a prisoner to things you can't change.'
> *Tony Gaskins, motivational speaker*

Week 40 Day 6

TIP Don't put toys and books in bed with your baby.

I advise they only have their bed toy (comforter) in their cot with them at nap time and at bedtime.

It might be tempting to pacify your little one at bedtime by leaving them with toys or books; however, it will have a negative effect on their overall sleep in the long run.

They have to know that their bed is for sleeping and not for playing. If your little one stays awake playing, they will become overtired and therefore emotional, finding it harder to fall asleep.

In addition, during the early hours, they might get distracted by a toy and wake fully, rather than dosing off back to sleep. Babies especially tend to roll around once asleep and if there are toys in the cot, this is likely to disturb them.

FOOD FOR THOUGHT Keep your baby's three milk feeds a day, as well as three meals, until they turn one.

41 Weeks Old

FACT The best essential oil for relaxation is lavender.

MINDFULNESS Try an essential oil in a diffuser when you go to bed at night.

FOOD FOR THOUGHT This Banana and Peanut Butter Ice Cream is a healthy but delicious treat! Peel a couple of bananas – I usually use one banana per person – and pop them in the freezer in a sealed freezer bag for at least two hours. Put the frozen banana in a blender and blitz for 2 minutes. Add a teaspoon of peanut butter and blend for a further 2 minutes. Serve immediately.

TIP If you haven't got one already, install a carbon monoxide alarm to detect carbon monoxide poisoning.

Week 41 Day 1

It's really grounding to put your bare feet on the grass. Do this now with your baby so they get used to the feeling and will enjoy walking barefoot once they are toddling. It's a really good sensory experience for you both.

Research suggests that this is a way you can connect to the Earth's natural energy and that it has healing powers strong enough to combat chronic pain and fatigue.

FACT Allowing your baby time without socks on will help develop their plantar reflex. Babies are born with this reflex; it signals to them to push away from objects that are near their feet.

TIP Make sure your baby spend lots of time without socks on so they can feel the surfaces they are on and are able to grip things with their feet.

Week 41 Day 2

FACT Babies use touch to understand the world around them, which is why they want to grab everything in sight!

Here are ten things I would love your little one to touch and feel before they turn one:

1. Sand
2. Water
3. Cotton wool
4. Leaves
5. A pebble
6. Foam
7. Felt
8. A book
9. An animal
10. Grass

ACTIVITY Cut a satsuma into quarters and put it on a baking tray or similar along with another whole satsuma. Sit your baby beside the tray and let them freely explore the taste, smell and touch of the fruit.

Week 41 Day 3

FACT Sweetcorn contains folate and potassium. However, in order for these nutrients to be fully absorbed by your baby's body, they need to be digested rather than passed through the body whole. The outer shell of sweetcorn is difficult for your baby to break down, therefore it is advised to mash or blend the corn.

ACTIVITY Give your baby a raw corn cob to explore through their smell, taste, touch and sight senses.

FOOD FOR THOUGHT Try these Sweetcorn and Courgette Fritters for a healthy snack for you and your baby.

Ingredients
150g sweetcorn
150g onion, roughly chopped
80g cottage cheese
110g self-raising flour
2 eggs
1 garlic clove
½ teaspoon baking powder
300g courgette, grated
3 tablespoons olive oil

1. Add all the ingredients, except the oil and the courgette, into a blender and blend. Then add the courgette to the mixture and combine.
2. Heat the oil in a non-stick pan and add 2 tablespoons of the mixture. Flatten with the back of the spoon.
3. Fry for a few minutes until they are golden brown. Repeat until you have used up all the mixture.

TIP Try puréeing sweetcorn and add it to your little one's dinner – they will enjoy the sweet taste!

Week 41 Day 4

Every night when you are putting your little one to bed, get into the habit of looking up to the moon and saying goodnight to the key people in your baby's life before drawing the curtains. It's a way of helping your baby stay connected to the people they love and letting them know that everyone is going to bed.

As your little one gets older, you can explain to them the concept that everyone you are saying goodnight to can see the same moon, regardless of where they are in the world.

FACT Research shows that smiling is contagious. So the more you smile at your baby, the more likely they are to respond to you with a smile.

FOOD FOR THOUGHT Try cutting sandwiches into finger shapes for your baby; this will make them much easier to eat. You can use a rolling pin to roll over the sandwich as this will help the bread stick together.

TIP I believe eating together as a family wherever possible brings you together and encourages little ones to copy you.

Week 41 Day 5

Your baby might be ready for their first haircut soon, so it's time to find a local hairdresser that caters for young children.

This may come as a surprise, but the shorter and finer your little one's hair is, the more I advise you to have it trimmed. By trimming their hair little and often, it will encourage stronger growth.

My tips for your baby's first visit:

- Make sure your baby isn't tired or hungry.
- Take their favourite toy so they have something to hold.
- Their natural reaction will be to brush away the feeling when someone touches their hair with the scissors, so if they are sitting in a child's seat, sit at the same level as them so you can chat to them and reassure them while gently holding their hands.
- They can also sit on your lap while you talk to them through the mirror and stroke their hands as a distraction.
- Discuss how you would like their hair to be cut before your little one sits in the chair, making their time in the chair not too long.

Week 41 Day 6

All babies learn gestures before they learn words. Big gestures, such as putting their arms up when they want to be held or shaking their head when they don't want any more food, are common. You can also introduce your baby to signing which will help your baby put meaning behind the words.

Signing is about enhancing, not replacing language. It should be used alongside speech so your baby can make the link between the gesture and the word.

ACTIVITY Teach your little one these three basic signs:

- More: show them how to open and close the palms of their hands.
- Drink: cupping their hand and bringing it up to their mouth.
- Please: touch their chin with their hand.

TIP Make sure your baby is looking at you when you are signing to them so they can focus on both the action and the word. Start with straightforward, meaningful signs such as 'bye bye', as these are useful for your baby in everyday conversations.

42 Weeks Old

FOOD FOR THOUGHT Brown bread is easier for your little one to eat than white bread. Once it is in your baby's mouth, white bread can become sticky and tricky to chew.

ACTIVITY Create a handprint keepsake with your baby. Get a piece of white card and washable paint, then create handprints. These cards are not only a lovely keepsake to remember how small they once were, but also great cards for family members. Add a copy to your baby's memory box.

TIP If they aren't opening their hands easily, try tickling the back of their hand.

Week 42 Day 1

FACT There are many benefits to your body if you stretch regularly: stretching lengthens your muscles; prevents aches and pains; improves physical performance; relaxes the body; and reduces the chance of injury while exercising.

MINDFULNESS Try this knee-to-chest stretch at home today – it will relax your hips, thighs and glutes while promoting overall relaxation. To do the stretch, follow these steps:

1. Lie on your back with both knees bent and your feet flat on the floor.
2. Keep your left knee bent or extend it straight out along the floor.
3. Draw your right knee into your chest, clasping your hands behind your thigh or at the top of your shinbone.
4. Lengthen your spine all the way down to your tailbone, and avoid lifting your hips.
5. Breathe deeply, releasing any tension.
6. Hold this pose for thirty seconds to one minute.
7. Repeat with the other leg.

Week 42 Day 2

Are you an 'I love you' kind of person?

Some people say it freely, while others rarely do, or only to a particular few.

I'm not saying that either way is right or wrong, but I would like you to think about how often you say it to your baby as I believe that children should be loved for who they are and not what they have achieved.

Whispering the words 'I love you' right before bedtime, no matter how your day has gone, is a lovely way for your little one to fall asleep.

Week 42 Day 3

The world is a big, new and exciting place for your little one and is full of surprises and opportunities for your baby to learn.

'In every walk with nature one receives far more than he seeks.'
John Muir, nineteenth-century naturalist and environmental campaigner

ACTIVITY Go on a nature walk and enjoy some fresh air with your little one today.

Find your baby a leaf to hold and show them how to use it as a fan, or pick a flower for them to sniff. Let your baby spend some time on the ground and explore their natural surroundings. There are lots of different textures for them to feel such as grass, leaves, pine cones, soil and tree bark etc.

Point out any wildlife you see such as birds, squirrels or butterflies.

TIP Be careful they don't put anything in their mouth that they shouldn't and take wet wipes or a bottle of water so you can wash their hands after their exploring.

ACTIVITY This is a painting activity which can be saved and framed to go in your little one's bedroom or playroom – it's a really lovely keepsake!

You will need:

- A piece of canvas
- Sellotape or masking tape
- Washable children's paint (and either a naked baby or a good long-sleeved bib)

1. Mark out the first letter of your baby's name (or their whole name if you have room) with Sellotape or masking tape on a piece of canvas.
2. Let your baby paint all over the canvas with their hands, a sponge or a brush.
3. Allow the canvas to dry, before peeling the tape off to reveal a clear silhouette of the first letter of their name.

Week 42 Day 5

ACTIVITY Use the plastic lids that open and close from baby wipe packaging and glue them to a piece of cardboard. Underneath each lid, glue a photograph of a family member or pet and write their name above it. Let your little one explore the board and get excited when they open a different person each time.

FOOD FOR THOUGHT Try this healthy, sweet treat for your baby today: a banana and Greek yoghurt sandwich, which is easy for them to hold and eat.

REMINDER Here is a reminder to take your monthly photo today of your baby alongside your chosen teddy bear. This is number ten of your twelve photographs, which you can keep to document your little one's growth during their first year.

300 days with your baby!

The bond between you as parents and your baby is the foundation for your little one's security, and will help them replicate this in their future relationships.

Your baby is more likely to become an affectionate adult if they are brought up in a loving and secure environment where affection is demonstrated as part of everyday life.

ACTIVITY Teach your baby how to blow a kiss when you say goodbye to people. It's a loving gesture that will get a great reaction from adults and takes a lot of coordination from your baby to learn.

43 Weeks Old

Looking in a mirror is not only really fun for a baby but it can help them learn to focus and track images. Seeing their reflection alongside you helps social and emotional development as your little one can see themselves interacting with you.

ACTIVITY Hold your baby in front of a mirror and talk to their reflection. Point to different parts of their body, naming their nose, ears, toes etc.

FACT Babies are born with 300 bones, but they will fuse together over time and by adulthood we only have 206 bones in the body.

Week 43 Day 1

ACTIVITY Thread three pieces of different-coloured material through three loo roll tubes and show your baby how to pull the material out. This will help your little one's colour recognition as you can ask them to pull a certain colour and show them which one you mean.

FOOD FOR THOUGHT Think about introducing your baby to different tastes from around the world. This will stop you repeating the same types of foods and expand their taste buds.

TIP When you leave your baby, whether it's to pop to the shops for half an hour or to go elsewhere for a week, always say goodbye and tell them how long it will be until you come back. Even if they get upset or clingy, it's much better that they know you've gone and that you left deliberately. It makes them feel much more secure and they know that nothing bad has happened to you.

Week 43 Day 2

As the days go by, your little one will become more and more vocal. This is a great time to start using flashcards to help your baby build on their vocabulary.

FACT Your baby's memory is improving dramatically now, so they will retain the words that they hear often.

ACTIVITY Sit on the floor with your baby facing you. Use flash-cards with simple objects on them, such as a cat or a dog, and hold them up for your baby to see. Name the object clearly and enthusiastically, and encourage them to copy you. Remember that this isn't a pressurised lesson and should only be continued if your little one is enjoying it.

TIP Words that have one syllable are easier for your baby to learn at this stage.

Week 43 Day 3

ACTIVITY For an easy sensory play activity, simply tip porridge oats into a bowl and let your baby feel the texture by picking up handfuls and individual oats. Add some spoons and little measuring cups.

TIP You may need to reduce your baby's morning nap to thirty minutes now. You can judge if you need to do this by how quickly they settle for their afternoon nap. If they don't seem very tired at 1 p.m., this is a sign that they are sleeping too much in the morning. It's better to reduce the morning nap so they benefit from a good afternoon one.

Week 43 Day 4

MINDFULNESS A happy household is one where you appreciate each other. Parenting is *hard* but try to focus on the benefits to it; going to work has perks but can also be stressful and tiring.

ACTIVITY When you say hello to people, try to use your hands in a waving motion, while saying 'hello'. Show your little one how to do this and they will soon start to copy you.

TIP Having the confidence to say hello to others is a great life skill for your baby. If your little one learns to engage with new faces, it will naturally draw people to them, bringing more conversation, socialisation, enjoyment and happiness.

Week 43 Day 5

ACTIVITY When you are cooking in the kitchen today, give your baby some pans and spoons to play with as their very own drum kit . . . This may get a bit noisy when the lids start being bashed together like cymbals, but it's a great distraction for them if you are trying to cook in the kitchen!

FOOD FOR THOUGHT This Hidden Vegetable Tomato Sauce recipe is a great way to introduce more vegetables into your baby's diet. You can follow the suggestions below or use whichever vegetables you have in your fridge.

Ingredients
a large glug of olive oil
1 large onion, chopped
4 garlic cloves, crushed
2 teaspoons dried oregano
1 red pepper, chopped
1 courgette, chopped
a handful of spinach or kale
2 carrots, peeled and chopped
2 leeks, chopped
3 × 400g tins chopped tomatoes

1. Put some olive oil in a large pan, add the onions, garlic and oregano and stir. Cook for a few minutes then add the remaining fresh vegetables, stirring to mix well. Sweat the vegetables for about 10 minutes.
2. Add the tomatoes then wash out the tins with a little water and add this to the pan, too. Stir well and cook on a medium heat until the vegetables are tender.
3. Liquidise in a blender and serve as a pasta sauce.

Week 43 Day 6

ACTIVITY Make homemade scented play-dough for your little one. This is a great activity for babies who like to put things in their mouths. While I wouldn't let them eat chunks of the dough, if they lick it there is nothing harmful in the mixture.

You will need:
240g plain flour
270g table salt
230ml water
2 tablespoons of olive oil
Food colouring and scents (see below)

1. Mix the first four ingredients together in a bowl until they come together as a dough (you may need to add a little more oil to get the right consistency).
2. Add green food colouring and dried rosemary to make green dough, and purple food colouring and lavender oil to make purple dough. You can add all sorts of colours and scents such as orange and lemon if you prefer.

This dough will make yours and your baby's hands smell and feel amazing from the olive oil and other additions!

TIP Wrap the dough in cling film and it will last for a few days (and more plays) in the fridge.

44 Weeks Old

We are all surrounded by technology and it's something I get asked about a lot, so I wanted to discuss it with you today.

It is said that more children can manoeuvre around a tablet than swim, tie their shoe laces or tell the time. So how can we stop our little ones becoming addicted to screen time? I think this starts at home, from as early as now – and it may make you think and perhaps modify your own habits!

Technology is part of our world now so it's no use not letting your baby watch any television at all. In my experience, children who are told they can't have something will only want it more in the long run.

Personally, I don't mind a television being on in the room, but I'm not a fan of little ones having a device where they are looking down at a small screen. If they have their own screen, they are usually holding it – this prevents them from playing with anything else, they're looking down in a hunched-over position and there is no social interaction. Whereas if the television is on, the screen is much further away and everyone in the room can comment or interact with the TV programme, making it more inclusive.

There are some brilliant children's television programmes if you seek them out, and they can actually be very educational. When watching television programmes with your little one, make sure that gentle tones of voice and appropriate language are being used.

Week 44 Day 1

ACTIVITY Yoghurt is perfect for your baby's first painting experience. It doesn't matter if the 'paint' goes in your baby's mouth, so it's a perfect first messy/sensory play. You only need two ingredients: yoghurt (natural or Greek) and food colouring. You can use a brush or their hands to cover the paper in bright colours.

TIP Don't use too much food colouring or their hands will be stained until bathtime!

REMINDER This is your reminder to write a letter to your little one to add to their memory box. This month's idea is to get a second copy of your baby's first passport photo to include in their box.

Week 44 Day 2

ACTIVITY Make a push-in box. All you need for this activity is an empty cereal box, and some penne pasta! You could also use straws, just cut them into short pieces. Poke holes, using a pencil or scissors, around the box and put pieces of pasta in each hole. Show your little one how to push and pull the pasta in and out of the holes. This is a great activity to give to your baby while you're cooking and in the kitchen together. As well as being fun, it helps their fine motor skills.

FACT At this age, your little one doesn't really have a full understanding of their own strength and isn't yet coordinated enough to control how hard they pat or hold onto things.

TIP Teach your baby to be kind and gentle when stroking their soft toys or any pets in the house (never leave your baby and pet unsupervised). Encourage them by holding their hand and showing them how to stroke and touch their toys, while saying 'gently'.

Week 44 Day 3

Just because your baby may not be walking, it doesn't mean they can't explore the great outdoors. Invest in a waterproof all-in-one suit and let your little one crawl on the grass and explore the world around them, regardless of the weather.

> 'There is no such thing as bad weather,
> only unsuitable clothing.'
> *Alfred Wainwright, fellwalking author*

TIP Buy a suit that covers their feet, so they don't end up feeling wet or cold.

Week 44 Day 4

Your baby will be naturally fascinated by animals. In the beginning, they may be a bit wary of them, but this is all part of their development. The more you familiarise them with animals in books now, the more comfortable they will be when they meet them in real life.

On outings, point out any animals you see such as dogs in the park or squirrels in the garden . . . moving objects are always much more intriguing than still ones!

ACTIVITY Singing the song 'Old MacDonald Had a Farm' is a great way to show your little one the different noises they make. Repeat the verse and include a new animal each time.

Old MacDonald had a farm, ee-eye, ee-eye-oh
And on that farm he had a duck, ee-eye, ee-eye-oh
With a quack, quack here and a quack, quack there
Here a quack, there a quack, everywhere a quack, quack
Old MacDonald had a farm, ee-eye, ee-eye-oh

Week 44 Day 5

FACT As your baby approaches their first birthday, they will begin to have less REM (rapid eye movement) sleep than they had before.

ACTIVITY The great escape! Lay some plastic animals on a tray or table and use a piece of Sellotape to tape the animal to the surface. Show your little one how to use their fine motor skills to peel the tape and release the animals.

FOOD FOR THOUGHT Frozen peas are a great snack as they are not only healthy, but also entertain your little one while they use their pincer grip to pick them up.

Week 44 Day 6

ACTIVITY Make your own ball drop for your little one to enjoy. Cut circular holes in the top of a shoe box lid. Show your baby how to drop balls into the holes.

TIP Keep your baby monitor on a low volume setting, so you can still hear your little one if they wake but not so loudly that it booms around the room. The sound of your baby crying can be a stressful trigger, so keeping your baby monitor on a lower setting means you can go to them without feeling anxious or panicked.

MINDFULNESS Put a really soft blanket on the floor by the side of your bed so it's the first thing you step onto when you get out of bed. When you get up in the morning, think about what the blanket feels like when you step on it. Wriggle your toes and do a big stretch.

45 Weeks Old

'Every baby needs at least one adult who is
irrationally crazy about him or her.'
Urie Bronfenbrenner, psychologist

ACTIVITY Kiss your baby. Cuddle your baby. Tell them why they are the most special baby in the whole wide world.

FACT This is my favourite baby fact of the whole book: kissing causes a chemical reaction in your baby's brain and boosts their oxytocin levels. Oxytocin engages feelings such as attachment and love. Kissing also causes a release of vasopressin, which bonds parents and babies together.

Week 45 Day 1

ACTIVITY Sing the 'Pat-a-Cake' song to your little one today. Encourage them to pat their tummy every time you say the word 'pat'.

Pat-a-cake, pat-a-cake, baker's man
Bake me a cake as fast as you can
Roll it, pat it, and mark it with a B
Put it in the oven for Baby and me.

FACT If you have stretch marks, they will likely fade over the next year. Nearly all women experience stretch marks in a variety of areas during pregnancy: it's completely normal and nothing to be ashamed of. Your body has grown a baby for nine months – that is no mean feat.

Week 45 Day 2

FACT Your feet contain 25 per cent of the bones in your body.

MINDFULNESS Use a tennis ball to massage your feet, to relieve tension and increase your circulation. Roll your bare foot over the tennis ball, applying pressure to loosen the fascia.

ACTIVITY Teach your baby to climb the stairs and, more importantly, to come down safely. The best way for them to come down the stairs is backwards on their tummy, with their feet first. This stops them from falling on their head if they slip. Teach them by turning them on their tummies and showing them how to slowly come down step by step. Talk to them, saying 'Turn onto your tummy' each time, and they will very quickly learn what you mean.

TIP Always stand behind them in case they slip.

Week 45 Day 3

Continue to sing songs and nursery rhymes daily with your baby to develop their listening skills.

Your baby will respond to the intonation and pitch of the nursery rhymes and songs you sing – don't worry, you don't have to be a good singer!

FACT Learning words through song is easier than learning through speech, due to the familiarity and the continuous repetition of words in songs and nursery rhymes.

TIP Choose nursery rhymes and songs that are particularly repetitive, which allows you to emphasise words over and over again, and add actions to the songs.

Week 45 Day 4

MINDFULNESS Spend a few minutes of the day making a 'win list' of achievements throughout the week that make you smile, such as getting out of the door in time, enjoying an early night or making dinner for your family.

ACTIVITY Play a chase game with your baby by crawling around after them; this will encourage them to move faster and bring them excitement.

TIP Board books are good for your little one to read and play with on their own as they can't rip the pages.

Week 45 Day 5

ACTIVITY Find a large whisk and put rolled-up cloths or muslins inside. Show your little one how to pull the material out – this will help improve their fine motor and problem-solving skills all in one. This is a good activity for your baby to do in their highchair while you are cooking!

MINDFULNESS Use a hand cream to give yourself a hand massage.

Week 45 Day 6

Check what's on in your local area for the next month. Your little one is now at an age where they can really enjoy seasonal activities such as sunflower farms, pumpkin patches and farm parks.

Having family days out marked in the diary is something to look forward to and a way of creating memories and traditions.

ACTIVITY Put ice cubes and water in a large freezer bag, then Sellotape each of the four sides of the bag to the floor or your baby's highchair tray. Show your little one how to touch, feel and move the ice blocks around through the bag.

MINDFULNESS Thinking about your happy place can help you feel calm and relaxed. Your happy place can be anything from a holiday destination to a familiar space you feel content in.

46 Weeks Old

ACTIVITY Have a bath with your baby today. It's a great bonding experience and your little one will love the closeness and one-to-one undivided attention. Use a non-slip bathmat and have your towels and pyjamas ready for when you get out. Add some bubble bath and show them how to make a beard on their face with the bubbles for a fun and sensory experience.

FACT Studies show that reading a book before bed can improve your sleep quality.

TIP Aim to read for twenty minutes in the evening before you fall asleep.

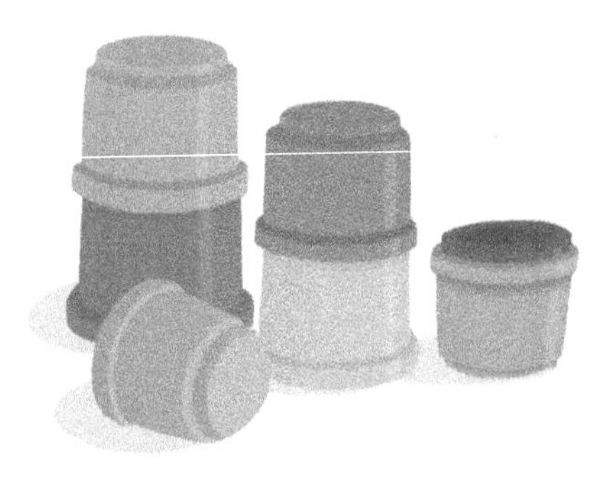

Week 46 Day 1

Now that your little one is more physically able, they will learn even faster through their sense of touch.

Books that include a wide variety of textures are good for them to explore. Describe each texture to your baby so they can start to learn the words to match, such as rough, smooth, shiny and fluffy.

ACTIVITY When your baby is in their highchair, give them three bowls of different textures to explore. In bowl one, put some mashed banana; in bowl two, add some freshly cooked pasta shapes; and in bowl three, put cooked peas. These are all safe for your baby to eat if they choose to put them in their mouth.

Week 46 Day 2

Arts and crafts activities are great fun for little ones so it's useful to start amassing a collection of art supplies that you can bring out for your baby on a rainy day, now and in the years to come.

ACTIVITY Start a collection for your baby's art and craft box such as: crayons, no-mess paints, paper, cardboard, tissue paper, biodegradable glitter, glue, pipe cleaners, milk-bottle tops, scraps of fabric and felt.

FACT When you display your little one's artwork, it's a great way to boost their self-esteem.

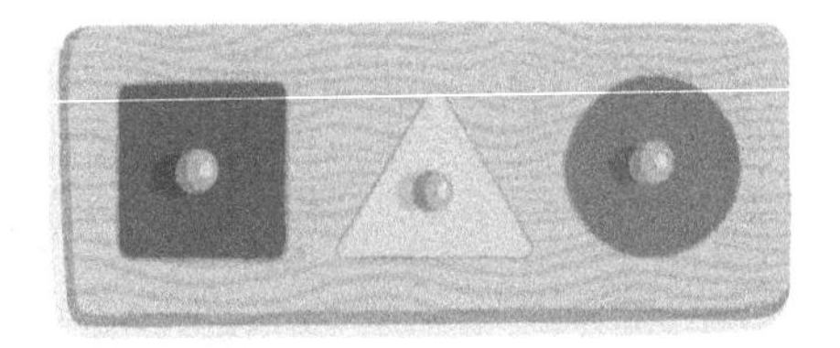

Week 46 Day 3

At this age, babies love playing in and crawling through tunnels. You can either buy one, or make one yourself out of cardboard boxes.

FACT Crawling through tunnels will help improve your little one's strength, mobility, spatial awareness and concentration.

ACTIVITY Open both ends of a cardboard box to create a tunnel for your little one to crawl through. Using the scissors, cut holes at the top of the cardboard box to allow enough room for you to thread different coloured ribbons through. Your baby will love crawling through the ribbons! You can also customise it by cutting peep holes in the sides so that your baby can peer through and see you.

Week 46 Day 4

Periods of fussy eating are common and actually a normal part of your baby's development as they approach toddlerhood. The good news is it will gradually improve for the majority of babies.

So what causes fussy eating? There can be lots of reasons, which include genetics or environmental factors – all of which we can shape and influence.

I really do believe a good relationship with food begins during weaning.

Here are my tips if your little one has started to become a bit fussy during mealtimes:

- Eat together – I can't stress enough how important I think this is. If you sit there watching your baby eat with nothing to do yourself, it puts pressure on them and increases your anxiety. If babies see the adults around them eating the same foods as them, it will encourage them to try different things.
- If possible, sit around a table so that you face each other when eating and don't have distractions around the room that your baby may want to get down to see.
- Offer small, manageable portions so your baby isn't put off or overwhelmed.
- Make sure your baby isn't overtired or overly hungry when they sit down to eat.
- If your baby refuses to eat what you've prepared, don't force the issue or get upset, just take it away without a fuss and try again at the next meal time with a fresh attitude.
- If they haven't eaten their evening meal, offer them a banana or some cereal after their bath to ensure they are not going to bed with an empty tummy.

Week 46 Day 5

ACTIVITY Make a fun film of you and your little one. Prop your phone up and flip the camera around so that you and your baby can see yourselves. Hold them in your arms and dance to a lively piece of music while the camera films you.

This is a piece of footage that you can keep and treasure forever.

MINDFULNESS Remember, fun is contagious – your baby will always pick up on your emotions.

'In the happiest of our childhood memories,
our parents were happy too.'
Robert Brault, author

Week 46 Day 6

ACTIVITY Count out loud when you walk up the stairs with your baby. This will help to build their number recognition.

TIP If your baby has dry skin or sore lips, put cream on them at night when they are going to sleep so it can soak in and is less likely to be rubbed off by them.

FOOD FOR THOUGHT Try drinking a mug of hot water with a teaspoon of honey, a slice of lemon and fresh ginger. It will improve the appearance of your skin and is a good source of antioxidants and vitamin C. It is also anti-inflammatory.

47 Weeks Old

ACTIVITY Pour some paint into well-sealed freezer bags – you can either use singular colours or mix them up to make a rainbow! Little ones love the texture and watching the paint move around in the bag as they touch it . . . And best of all, it's completely mess-free!

FACT During the first year of their life, your baby will at least double in size. In fact, during the first six months they are likely to double in weight! After two years, the speed of growth starts to slow down.

TIP This is another reminder to check your baby's car seat straps sit parallel to their shoulders when fastened. You may need to alter them as your little one is growing.

Week 47 Day 1

ACTIVITY Make a simple Cheese Fondue for the family today.

In a pan, gently heat 25g of cream cheese, 25g of butter and 50g of grated Cheddar cheese until it all melts, then stir together. Serve in a small bowl with toasted bread fingers or vegetables.

Your little one will love dipping food into the cheese and will be more likely to eat their vegetables.

REMINDER Here is a reminder to take your monthly photo today of your baby alongside your chosen teddy bear. This is number eleven of your twelve photographs, which you can keep to document your little one's growth during their first year.

Week 47 Day 2

Your baby's first birthday is fast approaching and you might find that family and friends are asking what your little one would like for their birthday.

Here is a list of gift ideas that I think are lovely for a first birthday.

- Books with a birthday message written inside
- Personalised hairbrush
- Shape sorter
- Wooden puzzle
- Pop-up tunnel
- Bubble machine
- Building blocks
- Train set
- Toy car
- Farm animal toys
- National Trust membership

TIP Instead of spending money on a present for your baby, you could plan a memorable family day out such as going to the zoo.

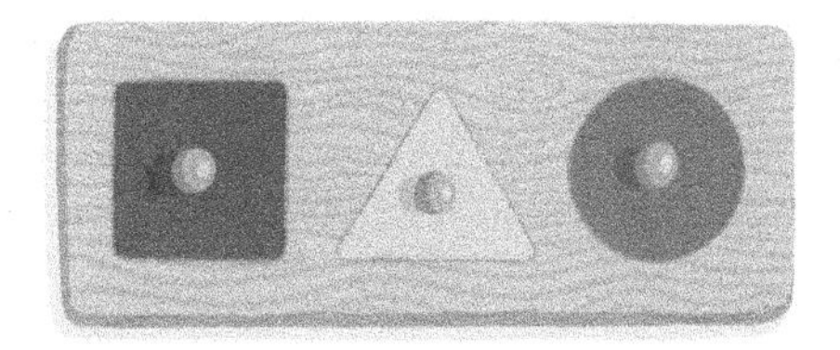

Week 47 Day 3

FACT Your baby is stimulated by songs with a fast tempo as it mimics their heart rate.

ACTIVITY Sing this 'Sleeping Bunnies' song and teach your little one the actions to match!

See the little bunnies sleeping till it's nearly noon
[lie down and pretend to sleep]
Shall we go and gently wake them with a merry tune?
They're so still, are they ill?
No! Wake up bunnies!
[jump up from the floor]
Hop little bunnies, hop, hop, hop
[hop up and down like a bunny]
Hop little bunnies, hop, hop, hop
Hop little bunnies, hop, hop, hop
Hop little bunnies, hop and STOP!
[show your baby how to STOP when they hear the word]

Babies love the excitement of the change in tempo of this song. It starts off quietly as you whisper while everyone is sleeping . . . then becomes faster and louder when the bunnies wake up!

Week 47 Day 4

ACTIVITY Start teaching your baby the names of their different body parts.

Rather than a structured activity, when you are holding your baby or sitting opposite them, put your finger on your own nose and ask them if they know where their nose is. Make it a game by tapping your nose, your head, your tummy etc.

You can take your little one's finger and touch their ears or chin, for example, and name the part you are pointing to.

Use this song to enhance your baby's understanding of the different parts of their body:

Head, shoulders, knees and toes, knees and toes
Head, shoulders, knees and toes, knees and toes
And eyes and ears and mouth and nose
Head, shoulders, knees and toes, knees and toes

Week 47 Day 5

ACTIVITY Find a tray that you can use as a designated play tray for your little one. The tray should have a solid base and be about 5cm deep so that it can hold tactile materials inside without them spilling over the edge. Use this tray to create sensory activities by filling it with a variety of different textures for your baby to explore. This could be anything from cereal to leaves and sticks found outside.

TIP If your baby starts to copy words but is pronouncing them wrong, it can be very sweet and funny, and it is tempting to adopt the same pronunciation when you are speaking to the baby yourself. However, you should still call them by their proper name, and not how your baby says them, so that your little one hears what they are trying to say in its correct form and their language skills improve.

Week 47 Day 6

FACT Organising gives you a sense of control, which makes you feel less stressed and anxious.

ACTIVITY Simply decluttering a drawer can give you a clear mind and a real sense of satisfaction and achievement. Why not pick one small area today and give it a thorough clear-out?

FOOD FOR THOUGHT Jelly is a light pudding, and good for anyone with a sore throat or a poorly tummy who needs some extra hydration. Buy the reduced-sugar packs of jelly to make with water.

48 Weeks Old

If your baby doesn't already, encourage them to pick up their beaker using two hands to enable them to drink independently.

If the beaker is turned the wrong way, show them how to turn it around in their hands. You can buy beakers with handles on them to make it easier for your baby to hold.

If your baby likes the game of tipping the water out (which many do), you can gently say, 'Na na na, we don't spill the water,' and turn the beaker the right way up so that they understand this isn't a game to play.

ACTIVITY Stick Post-it notes to a toy or unit and encourage your baby to pull them off. As they get older, you can use different colours and teach them to recognise the names by asking them to pick a certain colour, e.g. 'Can you pull the red sticker off?'

Week 48 Day 1

MINDFULNESS Mindfulness really is something that can be done while you are doing anything, it's just about being totally focused on specific tasks so that you are present in the moment, rather than your mind wandering to other places.

ACTIVITY When you read your baby's bedtime story, don't just read the words on autopilot, hoping to get to the end as soon as possible. Really focus on every word, the pictures and the storyline.

TIP Instead of throwing away empty bubble bath or shampoo bottles, keep them for your little one to play with as they make a great bath toy for filling and pouring.

Week 48 Day 2

ACTIVITY Sing 'This Little Piggy' to your little one as you tickle each of their toes. For the last toe, run your fingers all the way up their body and tickle them on their neck.

This little piggy went to market
This little piggy stayed at home
This little piggy had roast beef
And this little piggy had none
And this little piggy cried 'Wee wee wee!' all the way home

REMINDER This is your reminder to write a letter to your little one to add to their memory box. This month, include your baby's lock of hair from their first haircut.

Week 48 Day 3

ACTIVITY Cut out circular photographs of family members and put them in a cupcake tray, then place cupcake cases on top. Encourage your baby to remove the cases and reveal who is hiding underneath!

TIP Fix all units in your little one's bedroom or playroom to the walls. This will stop them toppling over on top of your child if they climb on a bookcase or chest of drawers.

Week 48 Day 4

Simple building blocks or a stacking toy will help your baby develop their fine motor skills, hand–eye coordination and spatial awareness.

It also allows your little one to work on their problem-solving skills by rebuilding a tower once it has fallen down.

ACTIVITY Help your baby build a tower and knock it down – remember, repetition is good!

FOOD FOR THOUGHT Add natural yoghurt to blended fruit and freeze in lolly moulds to make homemade milk lollies! Your baby can have these as part of their breakfast, as a snack or an after-dinner pudding.

TIP The milk lollies are a good way of encouraging your little one to eat if they are teething or off their food.

Week 48 Day 5

ACTIVITY Put together some story baskets to bring your little one's favourite books to life. Gather toys that are relevant to each story for your baby to hold and explore while you read to them. This creates imaginative play, encourages conversation and will help your baby fall in love with the magic of books.

Here are some examples:

- *Goldilocks and the Three Bears* – three teddy bears of different sizes plus three plastic bowls with spoons
- *Three Little Pigs* – toy pigs and some straw, twigs and building blocks
- *Dear Zoo* – toy animals and a basket with a lid
- *Fox's Socks* – different coloured pairs of socks and a toy fox

TIP Use a different voice for all of the characters and animals in the stories to help bring the story to life even more.

Week 48 Day 6

Is it time for a first pair of shoes?

It's best for your baby to learn to walk without any shoes on as their toes are vital in helping them balance. However, you will need to put shoes on your little one when they are toddling outside.

Remember that every child is different and will develop at their own pace. On average, most babies start walking between twelve to sixteen months of age, but I have had some who are running on their first birthday, and others who are only just taking their first steps at eighteen months old – this is all normal.

TIP I always recommend getting your little one's feet professionally measured to ensure the best fit so that their shoes don't rub or restrict their feet.

49 Weeks Old

Your baby's first birthday is just three weeks away so let's start thinking about how you will celebrate it.

Here are my tips if you are planning a first birthday party:

- Think about your little one's favourite book or character; you could plan the party around this theme.
- Create a welcoming atmosphere with bubbles and music.
- If you are planning a party, hold it in the afternoon so that you can prepare while your little one has their afternoon nap. They are more likely to enjoy their time with everyone after they have had their big nap.

A big party with lots of people might be overwhelming for your little one and a small afternoon tea party will be just as fun. You could also choose to take them out for the day. Don't feel the pressure to hold a party if you don't want to; your baby won't remember their first birthday.

TIP Ask a friend or a relative to be ready with their camera to take a photo of you with your little one and their birthday cake.

Week 49 Day 1

Some babies go through a phase of biting – some will give the odd nip and stop, while others become serial biters!

Biting can be a way of your little one expressing their frustration or it may be them just experimenting to see what their body can do. Some babies do it to defend themselves in a situation they don't like. Some use it to try to control a situation and others bite for attention. Your baby may also bite because of teething pain. If your little one has started to bite, try to work out *why* so that you can get to the root of the issue quickly and stop it happening.

TIP Biting is a phase that needs to be stamped out quickly as it won't disappear on its own. From the start, discourage them from biting by saying, 'Na na na,' and offering them a teething toy to chew on if they need it.

Week 49 Day 2

ACTIVITY This is a fun way to see if your baby is self-aware. Draw a dot on their forehead and hold them, facing outwards, in front of a mirror. If your little one reaches forward and touches the mirror, this is a sign they aren't yet self-aware. If they touch the dot on their forehead, then they are.

Don't worry if they can't do it now; they will learn in time!

FACT Your baby's eyes may still change in colour tone slightly. The base colour is usually set by nine months; however, subtle changes in tone can still occur at this stage.

Week 49 Day 3

If you are formula feeding your baby, you can wean them onto full-fat cow's milk as soon as they are twelve months old.

Make the change over the course of a week. On day one, make up 30ml (1fl oz) less than you normally would of the formula and add 30ml (1fl oz) of cow's milk to the formula. Increase this to 60ml (2fl oz) on day two and so on, until after a week you can just pour in the cow's milk straight from the fridge. Doing it this way means your baby gradually gets used to the taste without really noticing.

If you are currently giving your baby expressed breast milk but want to swap to cow's milk, follow exactly the same plan.

If your little one has been exclusively breastfed and doesn't take a bottle, I would go straight to a soft teat beaker rather than a bottle.

I always give children full-fat milk as opposed to semi- or skimmed milk as it has more nutrients and calories for healthy growth and development.

TIP Some babies will find the milk too cold to drink if it comes straight out of the fridge, so warm the baby bottle of cow's milk in a jug of boiling water and test the temperature to make sure it's not too hot on the back of your wrist before offering to your baby.

Week 49 Day 4

Babies sometimes realise they can get to places quicker if they crawl, so it is common for them to switch between the two for a while. At first, your baby will be a little bit wobbly on his feet and will probably fall down a few times. This is normal: falling over to a toddler isn't like falling over to us – they bounce a lot better!

Encourage your little one to walk by:

- Holding an enticing toy just above their eye level, so they look up and take a step towards it
- Showing them how to hold onto the handlebars and push a walker along
- Propping them with their back against the sofa and then sitting a metre away from them with your arms outstretched, encouraging them to take your hands and walk towards you

TIP When your baby is learning to walk, do what you can to cushion their falls, but allow them to fall when safe so that they practise putting their hands out in front to save themselves – it's a natural reflex we are all born with.

If you are thinking about your little one's first birthday, here's a super healthy idea for their first birthday cake . . . a fruit train!

You will need:

Watermelon
Cantaloupe melon
Strawberries
Grapes
Banana
Kiwi fruit

1. Cut the watermelon into two rectangles – this will form the front part of the train.
2. Cut the cantaloupe melon into two smaller rectangles and scoop out the middle to create two 'bowls'.
3. Fill these two bowls with chopped grapes and strawberries.
4. Slice the kiwi fruit and attach to the sides of the train using toothpicks.
5. Cut a banana in half and place as a funnel on the front of the train.

Week 49 Day 6

Be mindful that when you take your little one to new places, they might feel a bit cautious in new surroundings or when being introduced to new people.

The best thing for them is to learn from your confidence. Include them in your conversations. For example, when paying at the till in a shop, say to the shopkeeper, 'We ran out of milk so we had to come and get some, didn't we (baby's name)?' This means that all three of you are included in the conversation and it will show your little one that the situation is safe and not scary.

TIP When you hear unfamiliar noises, talk to your baby and explain what they are. For example, if an ambulance whizzes past, say, 'That's just an ambulance going to hospital, it goes *nee naw nee naw*.' If you are relaxed and smiling, your baby is much more likely not to worry.

50 Weeks Old

Even though it's important that you and your partner share the same values and views on the majority of parenting, you will both naturally be different in some areas.

Babies learn different things from each parent, so it's good for them to enjoy one-on-one time with both of you.

One of you may be quieter and calmer, while the other may be louder and more boisterous. Having sole attention from both parents will help your baby's emotional and intellectual development as they discover who they are as a little person.

'The best inheritance a parent can give his children
is a few minutes of his time each day.'
O. A. Battista, inventor

Week 50 Day 1

Your baby will now start to become more spatially aware and learn to understand the difference between big and small.

When you are playing with your baby, describe toys as big or small. Your little one will learn to recognise the difference between the size of their toys and be able to pass you the big or small toy when you ask for it.

ACTIVITY Introduce role play by holding up a teddy with a happy face and talking in a silly voice. 'Hello (your baby's name), how are you today? My name is (Mr Teddy) and I'd like a (cuddle, tickle, kiss)!' Play peekaboo with the teddy. Really softly stroke the teddy down your baby's cheek.

You might find your little one is very determined at the moment!

This determination is what encourages them to learn and develop new skills every day. Your baby may want to try and do things by themselves rather than accepting help, such as building a tower or unzipping a bag. Encourage them to keep trying by praising them and, once they eventually manage it, celebrate by clapping and smiling at them, saying, 'Well done!' This will really boost their confidence.

ACTIVITY Find a small, square-shaped cardboard box and glue a family photograph to each side of the cube. Show your baby how to roll and throw the box around – they will enjoy seeing the different faces on each side as it moves.

TIP If your little one goes off their food due to teething pain or illness, freeze savoury purées in lolly moulds and see if they will eat them this way. The ice lollies will provide hydration and much-needed nutrients to aid your little one's recovery. They are also a distraction if your baby isn't feeling very well.

FOOD FOR THOUGHT This Sweet Potato and Apple Ice Lolly is good for soothing your baby's sore gums. To make it, peel and chop up some sweet potato and apple, then put in a pan of boiling water to boil until soft. Drain, keeping some of the water, and blitz in a blender together. Add some of the water for added hydration. When cooled, spoon the purée into the lolly mould and freeze.

Week 50 Day 4

Your baby's imagination is starting to grow and they will love nothing more than if you sit down and initiate some wonder in a game or activity.

While playing, your baby can be who they want to be, and go where they want to go, so if you tell them that the red piece of Lego is a rocket, and the yellow piece is the moon, they can see that through their eyes while you make up a whole story of how the rocket gets to the moon.

This may look like a silly game with two pieces of Lego, but in fact they're learning new vocabulary, turn-taking and fine and gross motor skills, they're soaking up information about the world they live in and more importantly it's all done through play.

This type of role play will only grow and develop for your little one over the next year.

MINDFULNESS When you next have a negative thought, think about the 'magic ratio'. Research shows that it takes five positive thoughts to offset one negative one.

Week 50 Day 5

MINDFULNESS Positive affirmations are a type of mindfulness that utilises positive thinking and can be done absolutely anywhere. They are simple, short phrases that will help you overcome any negative thoughts you might be having.

Some of my favourite affirmations are:

- We are safe
- I am in total control
- I have time to prepare and decide
- I am patient
- We are not in danger, I am just uncomfortable
- I have many supportive friends who love me
- I am enough for my baby

TIP For a deeper impact, say your affirmations in front of a mirror while looking yourself in the eye.

Week 50 Day 6

FACT Your little one's feet will now be almost half the size they will be as an adult.

ACTIVITY Hang a mirror at your baby's height on their bedroom wall. As they look in the mirror and babble to themselves, this will help build their empathy, language and social awareness.

FACT Lentils are packed with folate, iron, potassium and fibre. Try your baby with some red lentil purée – lentils are delicious cooked with a little onion and a tin of tomatoes then blended until smooth.

51 Weeks Old

Create a checklist of life experiences that you can tick off with your little one as you do them together. Examples are:

- Go on a train
- Jump in a puddle
- Roll down a hill
- Paddle in the sea
- Build a sandcastle
- Bake a cake
- Have a picnic
- Ride on a bus
- Grow vegetables
- Build a den
- Go berry picking
- Run barefoot on the grass
- Make homemade pizza
- Run in the rain
- Build a snowman
- Skim stones and play Poohsticks by a river
- Make a mud pie
- Eat blackberries picked from a wild bush
- Blow a dandelion and make a wish
- Collect eggs from a chicken
- Read a book outside
- Pop bubbles
- Visit a castle

Week 51 Day 1

ACTIVITY Make your own ball tunnels for your baby today. This is a really simple yet great activity for crawling babies!

You will need:

- Large pieces of coloured card
- Sellotape
- Small balls, roughly the size of a tennis ball – ball-pit balls are perfect as they are lightweight and won't break the tunnels

1. Cut each piece of card in half lengthways and bend to make a U-shape.
2. Turn the tunnels upside-down and stick them to the floor using Sellotape.

Show your baby how to roll balls through the tunnels. They could also use cars to drive through the tunnels if they prefer!

Week 51 Day 2

ACTIVITY Thread three different-coloured materials through three loo roll tubes and show your baby how to pull the material out. This will help your little one's colour recognition as you can ask them to pull a certain colour and show them which one you mean.

TIP Although it's tempting, try not to interrupt your little one while they are focusing on something. Let their concentration come to a natural end before you interact with them. This allows your baby the time to process and problem-solve while boosting their self-esteem and independence.

The longer your baby can focus on something, the more successful they will be in achieving their goals.

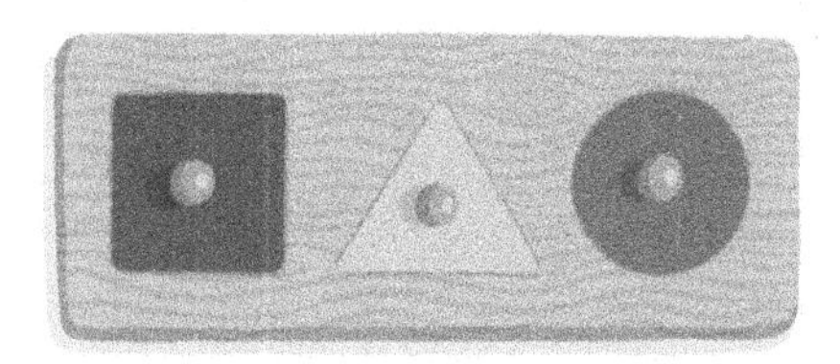

Week 51 Day 3

ACTIVITY Put three small books out on the floor and ask your little one to choose which one they want to read. See if they can pick it up and bring it to you.

TIP My golden rule for a good night's sleep is not to let your baby sleep past 3.30 p.m., so that they have a big enough awake window before you put them to bed for the night.

REMINDER This is your final reminder to write a letter to your little one to add to their memory box. You should now have twelve letters to cover the whole of their first year. Keep them safe and share them with your child when they are old enough to be interested!

Week 51 Day 4

In a few days' time when your little one turns a year old, they will be able to enjoy honey in their diet.

FACT Honey is a natural sweetener with anti-inflammatory and antioxidant properties, that also boosts yours and your baby's immune system.

You can:

- Add it to their porridge
- Mix it into their yoghurt
- Drizzle over a bagel or piece of toast
- Use it as a sauce to dip their fruit in
- Spread over their pancakes

TIP If your little one gets poorly, a teaspoon of manuka honey will really boost their immune system. You can add this to their breakfast or mix with warm water to offer them as a soothing drink.

Week 51 Day 5

It's time to start thinking about how your little one's routine will change over the next month as they progress onto Routine 5 – see page 393.

Soon they will drop their morning nap but keep their important afternoon one. Over the next few weeks, start to cut your baby's morning nap. First, reduce the nap time to half an hour and then just twenty minutes. It can sometimes take a week for your baby to get used to this. They may be tired and need to have an early lunch at 11 a.m. and be in bed by noon. Once they get used to their new routine you can gradually push nap time back to around 1 p.m.

Drop their 3 p.m. milk feed and replace it with a snack.

Continue to offer their morning milk until you notice them losing interest in their breakfast.

Routine 5

12 to 18 Months

At around thirteen months old, start to cut your baby's morning nap. At first, reduce the nap time to half an hour and then just twenty minutes. This can sometimes take a week for your baby to get used to. They may be tired and need to have an early lunch at 11 a.m. and be in bed by noon. Once they get used to their new routine you can gradually push nap time back to around 1 p.m.

The golden rule is not to let your child sleep past 3.30 p.m., so that they have enough time awake before you put them to bed for the night.

When you think your baby is ready (usually before eighteen months old), reduce their morning milk feed so they go straight into breakfast with a beaker of milk or water.

7.30 a.m. Morning milk/breakfast.

10 a.m. Snack.

Midday Lunch.

1 p.m. Two-hour nap.

3 p.m. Snack.

5 p.m. Dinner.

6 p.m. Bathtime.

6.30 p.m. Baby massage, stories, milk and cuddles.

7 p.m. Bedtime.

Week 51 Day 6

Now that your baby is about to turn one, I have put together eight milestones which you can tick off if your little one has accomplished them.

If they haven't reached all of them yet, I'm sure it's nothing to worry about, but it's a good idea to have a chat with your health visitor. Remember, every baby goes at their own pace.

1. Crawls
2. Raises hands to be picked up
3. Holds own bottle or beaker
4. Rolls a ball
5. Uses finger and thumb pincer grip to pick up
6. Rolls back to front
7. Waves bye-bye
8. Uses both hands to pick up an object

One Year Old

Happy first birthday!

REMINDER Here is a reminder to take your monthly photo today of your baby alongside your chosen teddy bear. This is number twelve of your twelve photographs, which you can keep to document your little one's growth during their first year.

Conclusion

I hope I have been a friendly and inspiring support to you each day while you have navigated your baby's first, and most important, year. I truly believe that a happy parent creates a thriving and confident child.

Small pieces of advice often make the biggest difference and I hope I've inspired you to create life experiences with your little one that will set the foundations for your future relationship.

Index

Page numbers in **bold** refer to illustrations.

INTRODUCING THE
MULTI-AWARD WINNING APP

LOUENNA

As seen in
OKAY! HELLO!
DAILY MAIL,
METRO & THE
TELEGRAPH

'Now parenting DOES come with a manual'

'The most rewarding £35 I ever spent! Amazing!'

'A complete baby bible, couldn't live without this now!!!'

Download Now

App Store
Google Play

The Norland nanny in your pocket offering 24/7 expert advice for a happy & thriving family...

www.louenna.com